ROMANTIC Crochet

20 BEAUTIFUL CROCHET PROJECTS WITH NATURAL COLOURS

EMMA ESCOTT

Tuva Publishing
www.tuvapublishing.com

Address Merkez Mah. Cavusbasi Cad. No:71
Cekmekoy - Istanbul 34782 / Turkey
Tel: +9 0216 642 62 62

Romantic Crochet

First Print 2020/ October

All Global Copyrights Belong To
Tuva Tekstil ve Yayıncılık Ltd.

Content Crochet

Editor in Chief Ayhan DEMİRPEHLİVAN

Project Editor Kader DEMİRPEHLİVAN

Text and Designs Emma ESCOTT

Technical Editors Rachel VOWLES, Leyla ARAS, Büşra ESER

Graphic Designers Ömer ALP, Abdullah BAYRAKÇI,
Tarık TOKGÖZ

Photography Emma and Robert ESCOTT

ISBN 978-605-7834-06-5

Thank you  for supporting this book with your yarn.

TuvaYayincilik TuvaPublishing
TuvaYayincilik TuvaPublishing

CONTENTS

PROJECTS

INTRODUCTION

I began crocheting at a point in my life where I was searching for a way to explore my creativity. I tried sewing, sketching and other crafts to little success. I began sharing these crafty experiments on a blog; Lululoves.co.uk, it wasn't long after that I discovered crochet. Once I'd mastered the basic stitches I began making whatever I wanted (sometimes to greater success than others) and found the freedom to create which I had been craving.

These days I still use crochet as a way to fuel my imagination. I am, and always will be, a dreamer at heart and I often find that I'm trying to evoke or re-create a certain feeling when I'm creating something. Crochet allows me to include my other interests: history and books, within my projects and I enjoy taking inspiration from vintage patterns and literature.

Crochet now serves so many purposes in my life; when I need to focus my mind I will follow a pattern, when I'm happy to let my mind wander I will sit with my yarn and hook and create freely, at other times I will crochet simply to relax and enjoy a repetitive pattern such as the granny square. I can no longer imagine my life without it.

I hope you will find something in this book to fuel your imagination. It's been an absolute joy to be able to create a series of designs inspired by the things I love to make. Inside you will find patterns for cushions, bags, simple garments and other accessories all using beautiful yarns in some of my favourite neutral colour palettes. I hope you find something that inspires you to pick up your crochet hook whether it's a simple face cloth set or a beautiful lacy shrug.

Emma

PROJECT GALLERY

Bloom Throw - **P.22**

Cowl and Wrist Warmers - **P.30**

Crochet Collars - **P.36**

Daisy Market Bag and
Water Bottle Carriers - **P.42**

Drawstring Bag - **P.50**

Shawl - **P.54**

Floral Face Cloth and Cleansing
Pads - **P.60**

Hand Towel and Cloth - **P.64**

Hot Water Bottle Cosy - **P.70**

Lacy Cocoon Shrug - **P.76**

Lacy Short Sleeved Top - **P.80**

Rambling Rose Cushion - **P.86**

Rose Bag - **P.92**

Round Rose Cushion - **P.98**

Ruffle Shawlette - **P.104**

Teapot Cosy - **P.110**

Posy Top - **P.114**

Vintage Motif Cushion - **P.122**

Materials & Tools

These are the materials and tools you will need for the patterns in this book. I've listed the tools I find useful but of course all you really need is a crochet hook and some yarn to get started!

Yarn

The following Scheepjes yarns have been used throughout this book and are suggested for the projects included in it. I hope you have as much fun discovering new yarns and colour combinations for your projects as I have in creating the designs for this book.

Scheepjes Merino Soft

Fibre content: 50% Superwash Merino Wool 25% Microfiber, 25% Acrylic
Ball Weight: 50g
Length: 105 meters; 114 yards
Yarn Weight: DK

Scheepjes Cahlista

Fibre content: 100% Natural Cotton
Ball Weight: 50g
Length: 85 meters; 93 yards
Yarn Weight: Aran

Scheepjes Stone Washed

Fibre content: 78% cotton, 22% acrylic
Ball Weight: 50g
Length: 130 meters; 142 yards
Yarn Weight: Sport

Scheepjes Soft Fun

Fibre content: 60% cotton, 40% acrylic
Ball Weight: 50g
Length: 140 meters; 153 yards
Yarn Weight: DK

Scheepjes Catona

Fibre content: 100% Cotton Mercerized
Ball Weight: 50g
Length: 125 meters; 137 yards
Yarn Weight: Fingering

Scheepjes Bloom

Fibre content: 100% cotton
Ball Weight: 50g
Length: 80 meters; 87 yards
Yarn Weight: Worsted

Scheepjes Merino Soft Brush

Fibre content: 50% Superwash Merino, 25% Microfiber, 25% Acrylic
Ball Weight: 50g
Length: 105 meters; 115 yards
Yarn Weight: DK

Scheepjes Our Tribe

Fibre content: 70% Merino Superwash, 30% Polyamide
Ball Weight: 100g
Length: 420 meters; 459 yards
Yarn Weight: Sport

Scheepjes Stonewashed XL

Fibre content: 70% cotton, 30% acrylic
Ball Weight: 50g
Length: 75 meters; 82 yards
Yarn Weight: Aran

Scheepjes Cotton 8

Fibre content: 100% cotton
Weight: 50g
Length: 170 meters; 186 yards
Yarn Weight: Fingering

Crochet Hook

Crochet hooks come in lots of materials the most common being aluminum, wood or plastic. Use the type of crochet hook you find most comfortable. The size of your crochet hook will determine the size of your project and how it hangs or drapes. Use the hook suggested in each pattern, check your tension (especially important for garments) and if necessary adjust your hook size accordingly (see Gauge/Tension in technique section.)

Hook Size Conversion Table

Metric	Imperial (UK & Canada)	US
2mm	14	-
2.25mm	13	B-1
2.5mm	12	-
2.75mm	-	C-2
3mm	11	-
3.25mm	10	D-3
3.5mm	9	E-4
3.75mm	-	F-5
4mm	8	G-6
4.5mm	7	7
5mm	6	H-8
5.5mm	5	I-9
6mm	4	J10
6.5mm	3	K-10 ½
7mm	2	-
8mm	0	L11
9mm	00	M/N-13
10mm	000	N/P-15

Tapestry / Yarn Needle

A needle with a blunt point and a long eye suitable for threading yarn is needed for weaving in ends and sewing seams.

Needle and Threads

To sew crochet (and other) embellishments to your projects – try to match your thread color to your crochet embellishments.

Stitch Markers

For counting stitches/rows and marking stitches. These are particularly useful when working in continuous rounds to mark the end of each round and to help you keep count of your stitches. They are also used in this book for marking stitches on garments and accessories when joining. You can use plastic or metal stitch markers but for crochet you must be able to open and close them. An easy (and affordable) alternative is to use a small piece of yarn in a contrasting color as a stitch marker.

Scissors

A small sharp pair of embroidery scissors for cutting yarn and trimming ends.

Ruler or Tape Measure

An essential for measuring those tension swatches!

Cushion Inserts

You can use foam, fiber or feather inserts for your beautiful crochet cushion covers, in this book I've designed cushion covers to fit 16" x 16" (41cm x 41cm) square inserts and a 16" (41cm) round insert.

Buttons

Buttons in a variety of sizes and colors are used for cushion backs and crochet collars. I have a jar full of pretty vintage buttons at home that I like to rummage through for projects!

Stitches and Abbreviations

Patterns in this book are written in US crochet terms, for equivalent UK crochet terms see table below:

US Terminology	UK Equivalent
Single Crochet (SC)	Double Crochet (DC)
Half Double Crochet (HDC)	Half Treble Crochet (HTR)
Double Crochet (DC)	Treble Crochet (TR)
Treble Crochet (TR)	Double Treble Crochet (DTR)

Stitch Abbreviations

bldc	back loop double crochet
blsc	back loop single crochet
bpdc	back post double crochet
bpsc	back post single crochet
ch (s)	chain (s)
ch-sp	chain space (the space below the chain stitches)
cl (s)	cluster (s)
dc	double crochet
fdc	foundation double crochet
fpcl	front post cluster
fpdc	front post double crochet
fpsc	front post single crochet
hdc	half double crochet
pc	popcorn stitch
sc	single crochet
ss	slip stitch
tr	treble crochet
rev-sc	reverse single crochet

Other Abbreviations

beg	beginning
dec	decrease
inc	increase
lp (s)	loop (s)
mc	main color
rep	repeat
rnd (s)	round (s)
RS	right side
sp (s)	space (s)
st (s)	stitch (es)
tog	together
WS	wrong side
yo	yarn over hook
{ }	contains additional information or clarification
( )	contains a group of stitches worked into the same stitch or space
[ ]	repeat instructions within brackets as many times as directed
* / ** / ***	Indicates start (and sometimes end) of a repeat, repeat instructions following * as many times as directed

Crochet Techniques

Any special stitches used will be detailed at the beginning of the pattern.

Slip Knot

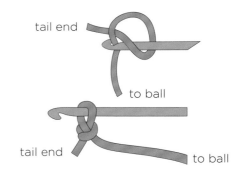

Almost every crochet project starts with a slip knot on the hook.
This is not mentioned in any pattern – it is assumed.

To make a slip knot, form a loop with your yarn (the tail end hanging behind your loop); insert the hook through the loop, and pick up the ball end of the yarn. Draw yarn through loop. Keeping loop on hook, gently tug the tail end to tighten the knot. Tugging the ball end tightens the loop.

Yarn Over (yo)

This is a common practice, especially with the taller stitches. With a loop on your hook, wrap the yarn (attached to the ball) from back to front around the shaft of your hook.

Chain Stitch (ch)

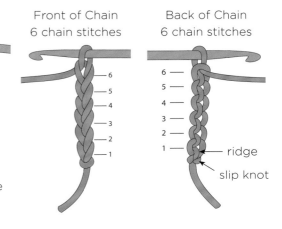

The chain stitch is the foundation of most crochet projects. The foundation chain is a series of chain stitches in which you work the first row of stitches.
To make a chain stitch, you start with a slip knot (or loop) on the hook. Yarn over and pull the yarn through the loop on your hook (first chain stitch made). For more chain stitches, repeat: Yarn over, pull through loop on hook.

Hint: Don't pull the stitches too tight, otherwise they will be difficult to work in. When counting chain stitches, do not count the slip knot, nor the loop on the hook. Only count the number of 'v's.

Slip Stitch (ss)

Starting with a loop on your hook, insert hook in stitch or space specified and pull up a loop, pulling it through the loop on your hook as well. The slip stitch is commonly used to attach new yarn and to join rounds.

Attaching a New Color or New Ball of Yarn or Joining with a Slip Stitch (join with ss)

Make a slip knot with the new color (or yarn) and place loop on hook. Insert hook from front to back in the (usually) first stitch (unless specified otherwise). Yarn over and pull loop through stitch and loop on hook (slip stitch made).

Single Crochet (sc)

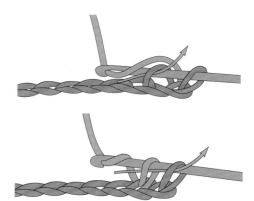

Starting with a loop on your hook, insert hook in stitch or space specified and draw up a loop (two loops on hook). Yarn over and pull yarn through both the loops on your hook (first sc made).
The height of a single crochet stitch is one chain high.

When working single crochet stitches into a foundation chain, begin the first single crochet in the second chain from the hook. The skipped chain stitch provides the height of the stitch.

At the beginning of a single crochet row or round, start by making one chain stitch (to get the height) and work the first single crochet stitch into first stitch.

Note: The one chain stitch is never counted as a single crochet stitch.

Half-Double Crochet (hdc)

Starting with a loop on your hook, yarn over hook before inserting hook in stitch or space specified and draw up a loop (three loops on hook). Yarn over and pull yarn through all three loops (first hdc made).

The height of a half-double crochet stitch is two chains high. When working half-double crochet stitches into a foundation chain, begin the first stitch in the third chain from the hook. The two skipped chains provide the height. When starting a row or round with a half-double crochet stitch, make two chain stitches and work in the first stitch

Note: The two chain stitches are never counted as a half-double stitch, unless specified.

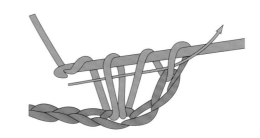

Double Crochet (dc)

Starting with a loop on your hook, yarn over hook before inserting hook in stitch or space specified and draw up a loop (three loops on hook). Yarn over and pull yarn through two loops (two loops remain on hook). Yarn over and pull yarn through remaining two loops on hook (first dc made). The height of a double crochet stitch is three chains high.

When working double crochet stitches into a foundation chain, begin the first stitch in the fourth chain from the hook.

The three skipped chains count as the first double crochet stitch. When starting a row or round with a double crochet stitch, make three chain stitches (which count as the first double crochet), skip the first stitch (under the chains) and work a double crochet in the next (second) stitch. On the following row or round, when you work in the 'made' stitch, you will be working in the top chain (3rd chain stitch of the three chains).

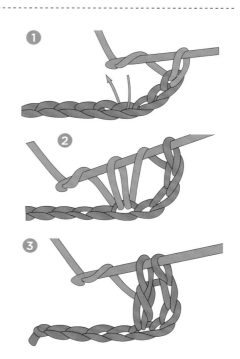

Treble (Or Triple) Crochet (tr)

Starting with a loop on your hook, yarn over hook twice before inserting hook in stitch or space specified and draw up a loop (four loops on hook). Yarn over and pull yarn through two loops (three loops remain on hook). Again, make a yarn over and pull yarn through two loops (two loops remain on hook). Once more, yarn over and pull through remaining two loops (first tr made).

The height of a treble crochet stitch is four chains high.

When working treble crochet stitches into a foundation chain, begin the first stitch in the fifth chain from the hook. The four skipped chains count as the first treble crochet stitch. When starting a row or round with a treble crochet stitch, make four chain stitches (which count as the first treble crochet), skip the first stitch (under the chains) and work a treble crochet in the next (second) stitch. On the following row or round, when you work in the 'made' stitch, you will be working in the top chain (4th chain stitch of the four chains).

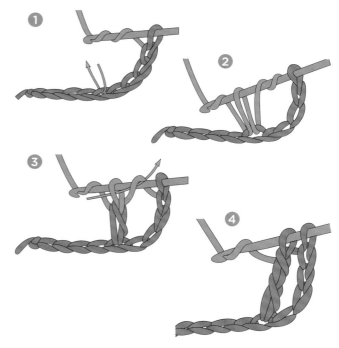

Double Treble (Or Double Triple) Crochet (dtr)

Starting with a loop on your hook, yarn over hook three times before inserting hook in stitch or space specified and draw up a loop (five loops on hook). *Yarn over and pull yarn through two loops; rep from * three times more (until only the loop on your hook remains (first dtr made).The height of a double treble crochet stitch is five chains high.

Turning Chains

The pattern will state whether a turning chain counts as a stitch or not.

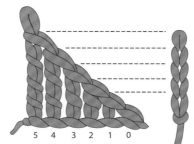

5	Double Treble Crochet
4	Treble Crochet
3	Double Crochet
2	Half-Double Crochet
1	Single Crochet
0	Slip Stitch

Magic Ring (or Adjustable Ring)

1 Form a loop with the yarn, keeping the tail end of the yarn behind the working yarn (the yarn attached to the ball).

2 Insert the hook through the loop (from front to back), and pull the working yarn through the loop (from back to front). Do not tighten up the loop.

3 Using the working yarn, make a chain stitch (to secure the ring). This chain stitch does NOT count as first stitch.

4 Work the required stitches into the ring (over the tail strand). When all the stitches are done, gently tug the tail end to close the ring, before joining the round (if specified). Remember, make sure this tail is firmly secured before weaving in the end.

Note If you prefer, you can use any type of "ring" to start your project (or start with ch-2, and working the first round in the second chain from hook). The advantage of using the adjustable Magic Ring, is that when it is tightened, it closes the hole completely.

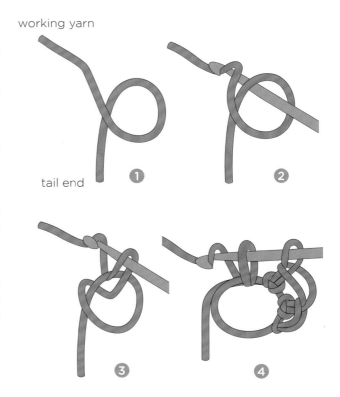

working yarn

tail end

Foundation Double Crochet

Ch4 (counts as 1dc, 1ch), yarn over, insert hook into fourth chain from hook, yarn over and pull up a loop (3 loops on hook), yarn over and pull through 1 loop (1 chain made), yarn over and pull through 2 loops (2 loops on hook), yarn over and pull through remaining two loops (first fdc created)

For Subsequent Stitches

Yarn over, insert hook under the 2 loops of chain at bottom of stitch just made, yarn over and pull up a loop (3 loops on hook), yarn over and pull through 1 loop (1 chain made), [yarn over and pull through 2 loops] twice.

Crocheting Around A Foundation Chain

When you want to start an oval piece rather than a round piece, start with the required amount of stitches in a chain. Single crochet into the second chain from the hook (if making an oval this will usually also be an increase stitch) and in each chain along. The last chain is where you need to put your increases (this will be indicated on the pattern) as you make the increases you will naturally turn to work up the other side of the foundation chain (this will be the other loop of the foundation chain).

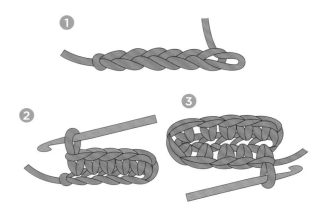

Changing Colors / Attaching New Yarn

With the current color, work the last stitch before the color change up to the last step of the stitch. Using the new color, yarn over hook, pull new color through remaining loops on hook.

New color / yarn

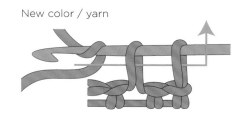

Back Ridge Of Foundation Chain

Most projects start with a foundation chain – a string of chain stitches. You can identify the front of the chain stitches by seeing 'v's. When you turn the foundation chain over, at the back are a string of 'bumps'. This is referred to as the back ridge (or back bar) of the chain.

When working in the back ridge of the chain stitches, insert the hook from front to back through the 'bar' (the 'v' is underneath the hook) and pulls the yarn through the 'bar'.

Working your first row in the back ridge of the foundation chain, gives a neat finish to your project. If you are seaming pieces together, it also creates a flatter seam.

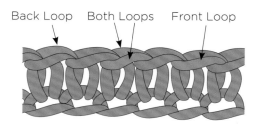

Front and Back Loops

Each stitch has an identifiable 'V' on the top. Unless otherwise specified, all stitches are worked by inserting the hook under both the loops – under the 'v'. Sometimes a pattern calls for stitches worked in either the front or back loops. These are the two loops that make up the 'v'. The front loops are the loops closest to you and the back loops are the loops furthest from you. Working in the front or back loops only, creates a decorative ridge (of the unworked loops).

Back Loop   Both Loops   Front Loop

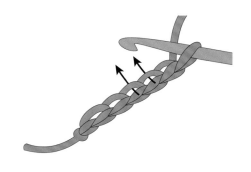

Blocking

To give your crochet creations a beautiful and professional look, it is advisable to block them all when finished. You can also block motifs before joining them together. Wet-blocking is done by pinning out your piece to size and shape (using non-rust pins) on a clean, flat and soft surface. You can use towels, foam board, or rubber mat tiles.

Depending on the yarn you used, you can gently wash your crochet pieces first and then pin them out, or you can pin out the dry pieces, and lightly spritz them with water, or (if they are NOT acrylic) hover a steam iron over them. Never let the iron touch the crochet pieces. Leave the pinned pieces to dry completely.

Crab Stitch

This stitch is also known as Reverse Single Crochet (rev-sc) and creates a neat edging to a project. It is similar to the regular single crochet stitch but is worked in the opposite direction - left to right (for right-handers) and right to left (for left-handers).

With a loop on the hook, * insert hook in next st to the right (or left for left-handers) and pull up loop, yarn over and pull through both loops on hook. Repeat from * across (or around).

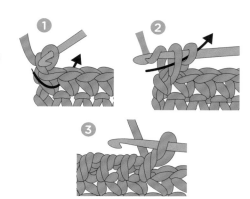

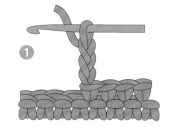

Picot Stitch

The picot stitch is mainly used as a decorative stitch for edging blankets etc.

Chain 3, insert your hook back into the top of the stitch you are working from, yarn over and pull through all loops.

Joining Seams

There are several ways to join seams:

1. Sew – Sew seams together using darning needle and matching yarn. It is advisable to pin your work together first so that the stitches and rows match wherever possible. The most common stitches are whip stitch or a woven stitch.

2. Crochet – You can crochet your seams together using a slip stitch or a single crochet join. Take care when joining with a slip stitch not to pull your stitches too tightly.

3. Join as you go – This method is usually used when joining motifs and is worked in the joining round by working slip stitches into the motif to be joined then continuing working the round of your 'working' motif.

Gauge / Tension

A gauge swatch is simply a way to compare your crochet tension to the designers to ensure your project comes out at the correct size. Always check your tension especially when it comes to garments and other items where size is important. To do this, read the tension instructions given at the beginning of each pattern and using the suggested yarn and hook crochet a swatch sample that measures approx. 6-8 in (15-20 cm) square. The pattern will usually give you a stitch and row count for a 4 x 4 in (10 x 10 cm) sample. Once you have completed the sample swatch measure 4 in (10cm) horizontally across a row of stitches and mark with pins. Note down the number of stitches between the pins. Repeat this process measuring 4 in (10cm) vertically across the rows and noting how many rows you have between pins. Now compare your stitch and row count to that given in the pattern.

Occasionally the tension instructions may give you a stitch and row count in numbers of repeats (multiples) - this is more common in lacy/complicated stitch patterns. In this case you will need to work a number of foundation chains suitable for the stitch repeat (for example if the stitch repeat is 12 stitches your foundation chain for your sample swatch could be 24, 36, 48 chains long) work your sample swatch following the main pattern, then measure the number of stitch/row pattern repeats (multiples) as per the tension instructions.

If your swatch does not meet the suggested tension for the pattern you can try several things:
• If you have too many stitches or pattern repeats in your swatch try again using a smaller hook.
• If you have too few stitches or pattern repeats in your swatch try again using a larger hook.

Fasten Off

To fasten off your work, cut your yarn, leaving an approx. 6 in (15cm) tail. Pull the yarn tail through the remaining loop on your hook.

Weave in Ends

To weave in your ends, thread your tail of yarn through a tapestry needle and on the wrong side of your work weave the yarn in and out of your crochet stitches.

Laundry Instructions

Always follow the laundry instructions given on the yarn label, as each type of yarn will have different properties. I tend to hand wash my crochet items and leave to dry naturally (blocking again if needed).

Tips for Following Crochet Patterns

• Read the whole pattern through before you start, paying particular attention to any notes at the beginning of the pattern. Make sure you are aware of any special stitches / techniques / abbreviations listed.

• Work and check your tension/gauge swatch – particularly for objects where size is important such as cushion covers and garments.

• Keep track of the stitch count for rows/rounds, especially if the round/row calls for increases or decreases. The stitch count is given at the end of the instructions of each round/row. Use stitch markers if helpful.

Abbreviations Used in Book

beg	beginning	**fpcl**	front post cluster
bldc	back loop double crochet	**fpdc**	front post double crochet
blsc	back loop single crochet	**fpsc**	front post single crochet
bpdc	back post double crochet	**hdc**	half double crochet
bpsc	back post single crochet	**Inc**	increase
ch (s)	chain (s)	**lp (s)**	loop (s)
cl (s)	cluster (s)	**mc**	main color
dc	double crochet	**pc**	popcorn stitch
dec	decrease	**rep**	repeat
fdc	foundation double crochet	**rnd (s)**	round (s)
RS	right side	**sc**	single crochet
sp (s)	space (s)	**ss**	slip stitch
st (s)	stitch (es)	**tog**	together
tr	treble crochet	**WS**	wrong side
yo	yarn over hook	**{ }**	contains additional info or clarification
rev-sc	reverse single crochet	**fldc**	front loop double crochet
ch-sp	chain space	**flsc**	front loop single crochet
[ ]	work instructions within brackets as many times as directed	*** / ** / *****	denotes start (and sometimes end) of a repeat, work instructions following * as many times as directed

Projects

Bloom Throw

Summer blooms have inspired this beautiful throw. It's the perfect project to pick up and put down as you please. I love the rhythm of a motif project as it allows me to daydream as I crochet. The Aran weight cotton not only means it works up fairly quickly but also gives it a good weight, making it a perfect lap throw for summer evenings outside or curled up in your favourite chair as the nights draw in.

MATERIALS

Scheepjes Cahlista, 100% natural Cotton, 50g/85m/93yds, shades

Old Lace 103 x 14 balls
Watermelon 252 x 3 balls
Sweet Mandarin 523 x 3 balls
Rich Coral 410 x 2 balls
Powder Pink 238 x 2 balls
Ginger Gold 383 x 2 balls
Light Coral 264 x 2 balls
Vintage Peach 414 x 2 balls
English Tea 404 x 1 ball
Brick Red 504 x 1 ball
Topaz 179 x 1 ball

5mm/US8H crochet hook
Blunt ended darning needle

MOTIFS

Shade Combinations for Motifs

Inner Shade Yarn A	Outer Shade Yarn B	Joining Shade Yarn C	Number of Full Motifs
English Tea 404	Watermelon 252	Old Lace 103	9
Vintage Peach 414	Watermelon 252	Old Lace 103	9
Brick Red 504	Sweet Mandarin 523	Old Lace 103	8
Topaz 179	Rich Coral 410	Old Lace 103	9
Vintage Peach 414	Powder Pink 238	Old Lace 103	9
Ginger Gold 383	Light Coral 264	Old Lace 103	7
Ginger Gold 383	Sweet Mandarin 523	Old Lace 103	8

Inner Shade = Rnds 1 + 2
Outer Shade = Rnd 3
Joining Shade = Rnds 4 + 5

Use leftover yarns in any combination of above to create 8 half motifs.

GAUGE

Rounds 1 – 3 of motif measure a circle approx. 4½" (11.5cm) in diameter using suggested yarn and 5mm/US8H hook.hook.

MEASUREMENTS

Finished Throw Measures: approx. 47 x 55" (120 x 140cm).

ABBREVIATIONS

Sp - space
Ch - chain
Sc - single crochet
Dc - double crochet
Ss - slip stitch
Rep - repeat
St/s - stitch/es
RS/ WS - right side / wrong side

SPECIAL STITCHES

Beg 3dc-cl - Beginning cluster

- Ch2 (counts as first half of first dc), *yarn over, insert hook into same sp, yarn over, pull up a loop, yarn over, pull through 2 loops, (2 loops on hook); repeat from * once more until you have 3 loops on hook, yarn over, pull through all 3 remaining loops.

3dc-cl - Cluster

- *Yarn over, insert hook into st, yarn over, pull up a loop, yarn over, pull through 2 loops on hook (2 loops on hook); repeat from * twice more, until you have 4 loops remaining on hook, yarn over, pull through all 4 remaining loops.

Pc - popcorn

- *Yarn over, insert hook in st, yarn over, pull up a loop, [yarn over, pull through 2 loops] twice; repeat from * four more times (making 5dc in the same st), drop loop from hook, insert hook from front to back through top of first st made, place dropped lp on hook and pull through st, 1 popcorn st completed.

Working Motif

- When joining, the working motif refers to the motif you are currently working on. Therefore you will be slip stitching into the motifs already joined.

PATTERN NOTES

- The throw is made up of 59 individual hexagon shaped motifs which are then joined using the 'join as you go' method in round 5. Eight half hexagon motifs are then added to the sides of throw using the same method. A simple border is added once you have finished joining. You may find it easier to make all your motifs up to round 3 first and then work rounds 4 and 5 when you are ready to join.

PATTERN STARTS

With yarn A, ch5, join with ss to make ring (or use a magic ring),

Rnd 1: Beg 3dc-cl, ch2, [3dc-cl into ring, ch2] five times, join with ss to beg cl - 6 x 3dc clusters.
Rnd 2: Ss into next ch2-sp, beg 3dc-cl, (ch2, 3dc-cl) in same sp, ch1 * (3dc-cl, ch2, 3dc-cl) in next ch2-sp, ch1; rep from * four more times, join with ss to first cl - 12 x 3dc-cl. Fasten off yarn A
Rnd 3: Join yarn B through any ch2-sp, ch3 (counts as first dc of pc st) *(pc, ch2, pc) in same sp, ch1, 1pc in next ch1-sp, ch1; rep from * five more times, join with ss to top of first pc - 18pc.
Fasten off yarn B.
Rnd 4: Join yarn C through any ch2-sp, ch3 (counts as 1dc) (1dc, ch2, 2dc) in same sp, [2dc in next ch1-sp] twice, *(2dc, ch2, 2dc) in next ch2-sp, [2dc in next ch1-sp] twice; rep from * four more times. Join with ss to top of beginning ch 3 - 24 groups of 2dc, 6 x ch2-sps. Do not fasten off yarn C.

A Note On Joining

Motifs are joined in round five by working slip stitches into the motif you are joining to (when slip stitching I insert my hook up from the WS to RS of motif). Working in the spaces between groups of 2dc, and into corner spaces. I like to join from right to left of throw so the row just completed is above the row I am working on, but feel free to use whichever way you find most comfortable. The complete motif is written below, as well as directions for joining your motifs along 1, 2 and 3 sides. Use diagram to see placement of motifs.

Rnd 5 - First Motif of Row 1 Only (complete motif)

Ss into next st, ss into next ch2-sp, ch3 (counts as 1dc), (1dc, ch2, 2dc) in same sp, [2dc in next sp (before next set of dc)] three times, *(2dc, ch2, 2dc) in next ch2-sp, [2dc in next sp] three times; rep from * four more times, join with a ss to top of beginning ch3.

Rnd 5 - Joining along one side to one motif

Ss into next st, ss into next ch2-sp, ch3 (counts as 1dc), (1dc, ch2, 2dc) in same sp, [2dc in next sp (before next set of dc)] three times, (2dc, ch2, 2dc) in next ch2-sp, [2dc in next sp (before next set of dc)] three times, 2dc in next ch2-sp, **(joining starts)**, ss into ch2-sp of motif to be joined, ch1, 2dc back into same ch-2 sp of working motif, [ss into next sp between groups of dc on motif to be joined, 2dc in next sp of working motif] 3 times, ss into next sp of motif to be joined, 2dc into corner ch-2 sp of working motif, ss into corner ch2-sp of motif to be joined, ch1, 2dc back into corner space of working motif, **(joining finished)** [2dc in next sp] three times, *(2dc, ch2, 2dc) in next ch2-sp, [2dc in next sp] three times; rep from * once more, join with a ss to beginning ch3.

Rnd 5 - Joining along two sides of your working motif to two motifs

Ss into next st, ss into next ch2-sp, ch3 (counts as 1dc), (1dc, ch2, 2dc) in same sp, [2dc in next sp (before next set of dc)] three times, (2dc, ch2, 2dc) in next ch2-sp, [2dc in next sp (before next set of dc)] three times, 2dc in next ch2-sp, **(joining starts)**, ss into ch2-sp of first motif to be joined, ch1, 2dc back into same ch2-sp of working motif, [ss into next sp between groups of dc on motif to be joined, 2dc in next sp of working motif] three times, ss into next sp of motif to be joined, 2dc into corner ch2-sp of working motif, 1ss into corner ch2-sp of first motif to be joined, 1ss into corner ch2-sp of next motif to be joined, 2dc back into corner ch2-sp of working motif, [ss into next sp of second motif to be joined, 2dc into next sp of working motif] three times, ss into next sp of motif to be joined, 2dc into corner sp of working motif, ss into corner sp of motif to be joined, ch1, 2dc back into corner sp of working motif, **(Joining finished)** [2dc in next sp] three times, *(2dc, ch2, 2dc) in next ch2-sp, [2dc in next sp] three times, join with a ss to beginning ch 3.

Rnd 5 - Joining along three sides of your working motif to three motifs

Ss into next st, ss into next ch2-sp, ch3 (counts as 1dc), (1dc, ch2, 2dc) in same sp, [2dc in next sp (before next set of dc)] three times, (2dc, ch2, 2dc) in next ch2-sp, [2dc in next sp (before next set of dc)] three times, 2dc in next ch2-sp, **(joining starts)**, ss into ch2-sp of first motif to be joined (previously joined motif of same row), ch1, 2dc back into same ch2-sp of working motif, *[ss into next sp between groups of dc on motif to be joined, 2dc in next sp of working motif] three times, ss into next sp of motif to be joined, 2dc into corner ch2-sp of working motif, 1ss into corner ch2-sp of first motif to be joined, 1ss into corner ch2-sp of **next** motif to be joined, 2dc back into corner ch2-sp of working motif; rep from * once more [ss into next sp of motif to be joined, 2dc into next sp of working motif] three times, ss into next sp of motif to be joined, 2dc into corner sp of working motif, ss into corner sp of motif to be joined, ch1, 2dc back into corner ch2-sp of working motif, **(Joining finished)**, [2dc in next sp] three times, join with a ss to beginning ch 3.

HALF HEXAGON

Row 1 (RS): Using yarn A, ch4, join with ss to create ring (or create magic ring), ch4 (counts as 1dc, 1ch), into ring work; 3dc-cl, ch2, 3dc-cl, ch2, 3dc-cl, ch1, 1dc, turn - 3 x 3dc-cl, 2dc.

Row 2 (WS): Ch4 (counts as 1dc, 1ch) 3dc-cl in ch1-sp, ch1, (3dc-cl, ch2, 3dc-cl) in ch2-sp, ch1, (3dc-cl, ch2, 3dc-cl) in next ch2-sp, ch1, 3dc-cl in ch1-sp, ch1, 1dc in 3rd ch of turning ch4, turn. Fasten off yarn A.

Row 3 (RS): Join yarn B to first st, ch4 (counts as 1dc, ch1), 1pc in ch1-sp (immediately after first st of row 2), ch1, 1pc in next ch1-sp, ch1, (1pc, ch2, 1pc) in ch2-sp, ch1, 1pc in next ch1-sp, ch1, (1pc, ch2, 1pc) in next ch2-sp, ch1, [1pc in next ch1-sp, ch1] twice, 1dc in 3rd ch of turning ch 4, turn. Fasten off yarn B.

Row 4 (WS): Join yarn C to first st, ch4 (counts as 1dc, 1ch), 2dc in ch1-sp (immediately before first pc of row 3), [2dc in next ch1-sp] twice, (2dc, ch2, 2dc) in next ch2-sp, [2dc in next ch1-sp] twice, (2dc, ch2, 2dc) in next ch2-sp, [2dc in next ch1-sp] three times, ch1, 1dc in 3rd ch of turning ch 4, turn.

Row 5 (RS): (Joining Round) Ch3 (counts as 1dc), ss into first ch2-sp of motif to be joined, 2dc back into ch1-sp of working motif (immediately after first st from row 4), *[ss into next sp between groups of 2dc of motif to be joined, 2dc back into next sp of working motif] three times, ss into next sp of motif to be joined, 2dc back into ch2-sp of working motif, ss into ch2-sp of motif to be joined, ss into ch2-sp of next motif to be joined, 2dc back into ch2-sp of working motif; rep from * once more, [ss into next sp of motif to be joined, 2dc back into next sp of working motif] four times, ss into last ch2-sp of motif to be joined, 1dc into last st of working motif. Fasten off yarn.

BORDER

Work one round of single crochet evenly around the throw as follows:

Rnd 1: Rejoin yarn C, to top right corner of throw [working first along short side of throw], 3sc into corner ch2-sp of throw, work along motifs as follows: 1sc into each st, 2sc into each ch2-sp, 1sc in joined corner sp, = 24sc for each full motif along short edge of throw. Continue along until next corner of throw, 3sc in corner sp. You will now be working along the length of the throw as follows; 1sc in each st, 1sc in joined corner sp of each full motif = 12sc for each full motif along length of throw. Work around half hexagon motifs as follows; 2sc around the post of each dc along edge of motif, 1sc into centre of magic ring (or joined ch4 loop) = 21sc for each half hexagon motif.
Continue working around blanket as above, join with a ss to beginning sc of rnd. Total stitch count for throw - 628sc

Rnd 2: 1sc into each st around, 3sc into each corner st of throw, join with a ss to beginning sc of rnd, fasten off yarn - 636sc

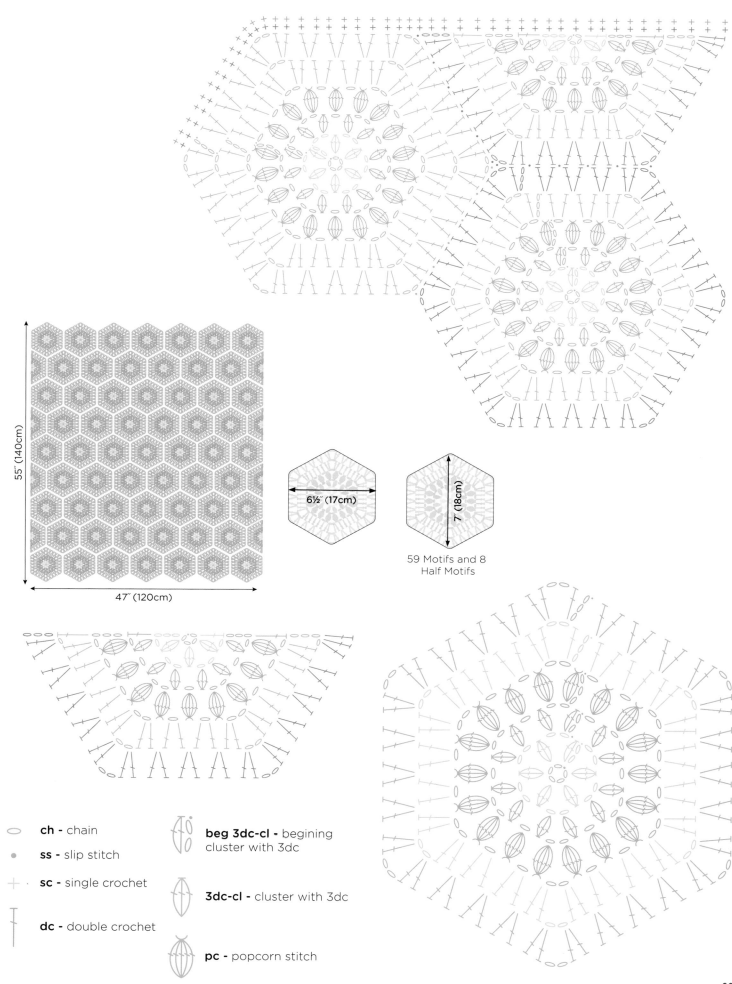

55" (140cm)

47" (120cm)

6½" (17cm)

7" (18cm)

59 Motifs and 8
Half Motifs

⬭ **ch -** chain

● **ss -** slip stitch

✛ **sc -** single crochet

✝ **dc -** double crochet

beg 3dc-cl - begining
cluster with 3dc

3dc-cl - cluster with 3dc

pc - popcorn stitch

Cowl and Wrist Warmers

Soft Merino yarn makes this cowl and wrist warmers perfect for staying cosy during the colder months while the crossed stitches add a lovely texture.

COWL

MATERIALS

Scheepjes Merino Soft, 50% superwash Merino wool, 25% microfibre, 25% acrylic, 50g/105m/114yds

Yarn A: Raphael 602 x 2 balls
Yarn B: Bennett 633 x 1 ball (25g used)

Scheepjes Merino Soft Brush, 50% superwash Merino wool, 25% microfibre, 25% acrylic, 50g/105m/114yds

Yarn C: Van Der Leck 257 x 1 ball (25g used)

4mm/G-6 crochet hook

Blunt ended darning needle

GAUGE

14 sts and 10 rows (3.5 st repeats) to measure
4 x 4" (10 x 10cm) square using 4mm/G-6 hook or size required to obtain gauge.

MEASUREMENTS

Finished Cowl Measures: approx. 14 x 11½" (35 x 29cm)

Total Circumference: 23" (59cm)

WRIST WAMMERS

MATERIALS

Scheepjes Merino Soft, 50% superwash Merino wool, 25% microfibre, 25% acrylic, 50g/105m/114yds

Yarn A: Raphael 602 x 1 ball (20g used)
Yarn B: Bennett 633 x 1 ball (15g used)

Scheepjes Merino Soft Brush, 50% superwash Merino wool, 25% microfibre, 25% acrylic, 50g/105m/114yds

Yarn C: Van Der Leck 257 x 1 ball (15g used)

4mm/G-6 crochet hook

Blunt ended darning needle

GAUGE

14 sts and 10 rows (3.5 st repeats) to measure
4 x 4" (10 x 10cm) square using 4mm/G-6 hook or size required to obtain gauge.

MEASUREMENTS

Circumference: 7" (18cm)

Height: 7" (18cm)

COWL

ABBREVIATIONS

Sp/s - space/s
Ch - chain
Sc – single crochet
Dc – double crochet
Fdc – Foundation Double Crochet
Ss – slip stitch
Rep – repeat
Rnd - round
St/s – stitch/es

SPECIAL STITCHES

Shell

- (1dc, ch1, 1dc, ch1, 1dc) in ch1-sp (centre of crossed dc)

Foundation Double Crochet (Fdc)

- Ch4 (counts as 1dc, 1ch), yarn over, insert hook in fourth chain from hook, yarn over and pull up loop (3 loops on hook), yarn over and pull through one loop (1 chain made), yarn over and pull through two loops (2 loops on hook), yarn over and pull through remaining two loops (fdc created)

For Subsequent Stitches

- Yarn over, insert hook under the two loops of chain at bottom of stitch just made, yarn over and pull up loop (3 loops on hook), yarn over and pull through one loop (1 chain made), [yarn over and pull through 2 loops] twice.

PATTERN NOTES

- Cowl is worked in the round by joining the first row of foundation double crochets with a slip stitch. Stitch pattern is worked in multiples of 4.

PATTERN STARTS

Row 1: With yarn A, 80 fdc (see special stitches), ss to top of beginning ch 4 to create round.
Rnd 2: Ch4 (counts as 1dc, 1ch), 1dc back into previous st (creates first crossed dc), * skip next unworked st, 1dc in next st, ch1, 1dc into skipped st; rep from * around, ss into 3rd of beginning ch 4. Do not turn.
Rnd 3: Ss into next ch1-sp, ch1 (does not count as st) 1sc in ch1-sp, *skip next 2 sts, 1Shell in next ch1-sp (centre of crossed dc), skip 2 sts, 1sc in next ch1-sp; rep from * along, join with ss to first sc. Do not turn.
Rnd 4: Ss into sp between sc and next dc, ch4 (counts as 1dc, 1ch), 1dc back into sp between sc and previous dc (working crossed dc around sc), * skip (1dc, ch1, 1dc), 1dc in next ch1-sp, ch1, 1dc back into previous ch1-sp (working crossed dc around middle st of Shell), skip 2

sts, 1dc in sp between sc and next dc, ch1, 1dc back into sp before sc (working crossed dc around sc); rep from * around to last Shell, skip (1dc, ch1, 1dc), 1dc in next ch1-sp, ch1, 1dc back into previous ch1-sp (working crossed dc around middle st of Shell), skip 2 sts, join with ss to 3rd of beginning ch4. Do not turn.
Rnds 3 and 4 form pattern and are repeated.
Rnd 5: Repeat rnd 3, switch to yarn B.
Rnd 6: Repeat rnd 4.
Rnd 7: Repeat rnd 3, switch to yarn A.
Rnd 8: Repeat rnd 4.
Rnd 9: Repeat rnd 3.
Rnd 10: Repeat rnd 4.
Rnd 11: Repeat rnd 3, switch to yarn C.
Rnd 12: Repeat rnd 4.
Rnd 13: Repeat rnd 3, switch to yarn A.
Rnd 14: Repeat rnd 4.
Rnd 15: Repeat rnd 3.
Rnd 16: Repeat rnd 4.
Rnd 17: Repeat rnd 3, switch to yarn B.
Rnd 18: Repeat rnd 4.
Rnd 19: Repeat rnd 3, switch to yarn A.
Rnd 20: Repeat rnd 4.
Rnd 21: Repeat rnd 3.
Rnd 22: Repeat rnd 4.
Rnd 23: Repeat rnd 3, switch to yarn C.
Rnd 24: Repeat rnd 4.
Rnd 25: Repeat rnd 3, switch to yarn A.
Rnd 26: Repeat rnd 4.
Rnd 27: Repeat rnd 3.
Rnd 28: Repeat rnd 4.
Rnd 29: Repeat rnd 3, switch to yarn B.
Rnd 30: Repeat rnd 4.
Rnd 31: Repeat rnd 3, switch to yarn A.
Rnd 32: Repeat rnd 4.
Rnd 33: Repeat rnd 3.
Rnd 34: Repeat rnd 4.
Rnd 35: Repeat rnd 3.
Fasten off, weave in ends.

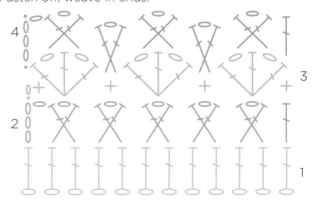

⬭ **ch -** chain

• **sl st -** slip stitch

+ **sc -** single crochet

⌶ **dc -** double crochet

⌶ **fdc -** foundation double crochet

WRIST WARMERS

ABBREVIATIONS

Sp/s - space/s
Ch - chain
Sc – single crochet
Dc – double crochet
Fdc – foundation double crochet
Yo - yarn over
Rep – repeat
St/s – stitch/es

SPECIAL STITCHES

Foundation Double Crochet (Fdc)

- Ch4 (counts as 1dc, 1ch), yarn over, insert hook into fourth chain from hook, yarn over and pull up a loop (3 loops on hook), yarn over and pull through 1 loop (1 chain made), yarn over and pull through 2 loops (2 loops on hook), yarn over and pull through remaining two loops (fdc created)

For Subsequent Stitches

- Yarn over, insert hook under the 2 loops of chain at bottom of stitch just made, yarn over and pull up a loop (3 loops on hook), yarn over and pull through 1 loop (1 chain made), [yarn over and pull through 2 loops] twice.

Shell

- (1dc, ch1, 1dc, ch1, 1dc) in ch1-sp (centre of crossed dc)

PATTERN NOTES

- Wrist warmers are made of flat square pieces of crochet, which are then joined along the side, leaving an opening for the thumb.
- To change yarn color, work last pull through of last st in the color required for the next stitch.

PATTERN STARTS

Wrist Warmer (make two the same)
Row 1: With yarn A, make 24 fdc, turn. Switch to yarn B.
Rnd 2: Ch3 (counts as 1dc here and throughout) *skip 1 st, 1dc in next st, ch1, 1dc back into skipped st; starting in next unworked st, rep from * to last st, 1dc in last st, turn - 11 crossed dc and 2 dc - or total of 24dc.
Rnd 3: Ch1 (does not count as st here and throughout) 1sc in same st, * skip next st, 1Shell in ch1-sp of crossed dc, skip 2 sts, 1sc in next ch1-sp, skip next st; rep from * around ending with 1sc in last st, turn - 6 shells, 7sc. Switch to yarn A.

Rnd 4: Ch3, * skip (1dc, ch1, 1dc), 1dc in next ch1-sp, ch1, 1dc back into skipped ch1-sp (working crossed dc around middle st of shell), skip 2 sts, 1dc in space between sc and next dc, ch1, 1dc back into space before sc (working crossed dc around sc); rep from * four more times, skip (1dc, ch1, 1dc), 1dc in next ch1-sp, ch1, 1dc back into skipped ch1-sp, 1dc in last st, turn - 11 crossed dc and 2 dc - or total of 24dc.
Rows 3 and 4 form pattern and are repeated.
Row 5: Rep row 3, switch to yarn C.
Row 6: Rep row 4.
Row 7: Rep row 3, switch to yarn A.
Row 8: Rep row 4.
Row 9: Rep row 3, switch to yarn B.
Row 10: Rep row 4.
Row 11: Rep row 3, switch to yarn A.
Row 12: Rep row 4.
Row 13: Rep row 3, switch to yarn C.
Row 14: Rep row 4.
Row 15: Rep row 3, switch to yarn A.
Row 16: Rep row 4.
Row 17: Rep row 3.
Use tails of yarn to sew wrist warmers together leaving approx 4cm / 1½in for thumb opening – see diagram. Weave in ends.
Using yarn A and with right side facing, work 16sc evenly around thumbhole.

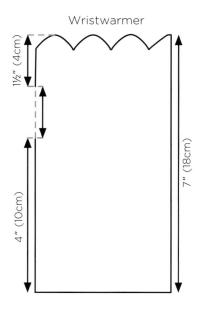

Wristwarmer

Crochet Collars

Crochet collars are a perfect quick make and are brilliant for giving old garments a new life. I've created two collars using one basic pattern here, one with a beautiful lacy border and another, which can be transformed into a statement piece with the addition of crochet roses and leaves.

MATERIALS

Scheepjes Cotton 8, 100% cotton, 50g/170m/186yds

Yarn A: 700 Light Grey x 1 ball
Yarn B: 671 Rust x 1 ball
Yarn C: 722 Ocre x 1 ball
Yarn D: 529 Violet x 1 ball
Yarn E: 717 Bordeaux x 1 ball
Yarn F: 713 Dark Green x 1 ball

NB: 1 ball each (of yarn A and B) is more than enough to make both collars. Yarns C to F use less than 5g each to make roses and leaves.

3mm/US3 crochet hook
Blunt ended darning needle
1 button approx ⅜" (1cm) if desired
Needle and thread

GAUGE

19 sts x 9 rows worked in double crochet to measure 4 x 4" (10cm x 10cm) square using suggested yarn and 3mm/US3 hook.

MEASUREMENTS

Finished Collars Measure: approx. 18" (46cm) diameter to fit a 16-17" (40-43cm) neck opening.

ABBREVIATIONS

Ch - chain
Sc - single crochet
Dc - double crochet
Tr - treble crochet
Ss - slip stitch
Rep - repeat
St/s - stitch/es

SPECIAL STITCHES

Dc2tog

– In this pattern the decreases are worked at the beginning and end of the rows.

To Work A Dc2tog At The Beginning Of The Row

- ch2 (counts as the first half of dc), yarn over, insert hook into next stitch, yarn over, pull up a loop (3 lps on hook), yarn over, pull through 2 loops on hook, yarn over, pull through remaining 2 loops on hook.

To Work A dc2tog At The End Of The Row

- Yarn over, insert hook into next stitch, yarn over, pull up a loop, (3 loops on hook) yarn over, pull through 2 loops on hook, (2 loops on hook), yarn over, insert hook into next stitch, yarn over, pull up a loop, (4 loops on hook), yarn over, pull through 2 loops on hook (3 loops on hook), yarn over, pull through all 3 remaining loops on hook.

Reverse Single Crochet - Rev-sc

– Backwards sc. Worked as a normal sc but is worked in reverse back along the row you have just finished. Insert hook into previous stitch, from front to back, pull up a loop, yarn over, pull through both loops on hook.

Picot

- Ch3, ss back into sc at base of ch.

PATTERN NOTES

- Main part of collar is the same for design A and B. Edgings and decorations are added after. You can add to the length of your collar by adding to the foundation chain in multiples of 7.

PATTERN STARTS

FLORAL COLLAR

Row 1: Using yarn A, ch87 (counts as 84ch, 1dc) 1dc into fifth ch from hook, 1dc in each ch along, turn - 84 sts.
Row 2: Dc2tog (see Special Stitches) 4dc, 2dc in next st, [6dc, 2dc in next st] to last 7 sts, 5dc, dc2tog, turn - 93 sts.
Row 3: Dc2tog, 4dc, 2dc in next st, [7dc, 2dc in next st] to last 6 sts, 4dc, dc2tog, turn - 102 sts.

Row 4: Dc2tog, 3dc, 2dc in next st, [8dc, 2dc in next st] to last 6 sts, 4dc, dc2tog, turn - 111 sts.
Row 5: Dc2tog, 3dc, 2dc in next st, [9dc, 2dc in next st] to last 5 sts, 3dc, dc2tog, turn - 120 sts.
Fasten off yarn A.
Row 6: Re-join yarn A to side of beginning ch 3 from row 1, ch1 (does not count as st) work 10sc along short side of collar (working around sts, 2sc on each row), 1sc in of next 120 sts, work 10sc along next short side of collar (working around sts, 2sc on each row) - 140 sts.
Fasten off yarn A.
Row 7: Without turning collar attach yarn B to first remaining foundation chain loop, ch1 (does not count as st), work 1 rev-sc (see Special Stitches) into last sc of row 6, 1 rev-sc into each st along collar to last st, ss into remaining ch lp of last foundation ch - 140 rev-sc.
Attach a 1cm/⅜ in button to one side of collar (to be fastened between dc sts on other side of collar) or, if prefered, crochet ties by attaching yarn B to top of collar, working a sc over the final reverse sc of row 7, ch40. Repeat on other side, fasten off and weave in ends.

ROSES (MAKE 6)

Make two in each of yarns C, D and E.

Ch11, 1sc in second ch from hook, 2hdc in next st, 2dc in each of next 7 ch, (2dc, 1ss) in last ch. Fasten off leaving 15cm/5in tail for sewing.

To make roses, roll up the piece of crochet around itself, starting from beginning single crochet, using yarn tail to stitch in place with a few stitches through the center of the rose. Weave in ends.

LEAVES (MAKE 2)

Using yarn F, ch8, 2dc in fourth ch from hook, 1dc in next ch, 1hdc in next ch, 1sc in next ch, ss in next ch, ch1 (working back along row into remaining loops of foundation ch) 1ss in same ch, 1sc in next ch, 1hdc in next ch, 1dc in next ch, 2dc in last ch, join with a ss to beginning ch. Fasten off leaving 15cm/5in tail for sewing. Weave in ends.

TO FINISH

Attach roses and leaves to collar with a needle and thread, using photo as a guide.

LACE EDGED COLLAR

Using Yarn A, repeat rows 1 – 4 of Floral Collar, fasten off yarn A.

Row 5: Join yarn B to first st of row 4, ch1 (does not count as st), 1sc in same st, *ch1, skip 4 sts, (1tr, ch1) 7 times in next st, skip 4 sts, 1sc in next st; repeat from * along. Fasten off yarn B.

Row 6: Re-join yarn B to top of short side of collar (through remaining ch loop at bottom of st from row 1), ch1 (does not count as st), 8sc along short side of collar (working around sts, 2sc for each row), 1sc in next st, *1sc in ch1-sp, [1sc in next st, (1sc, picot) in next ch1-sp] 6 times, 1sc in next st, 1sc in ch1-sp, (1sc, picot) in next st; repeat from * 9 more times, 1sc in ch1-sp, [1sc in next st, (1sc, picot) in next ch1-sp] 6 times, 1sc in next st, 1sc in ch1-sp, 1sc in last st of row 5, work 8sc evenly along short side of collar (working around sts, 2sc for each row), ss into remaining ch loop of foundation ch. Fasten off weave in ends.

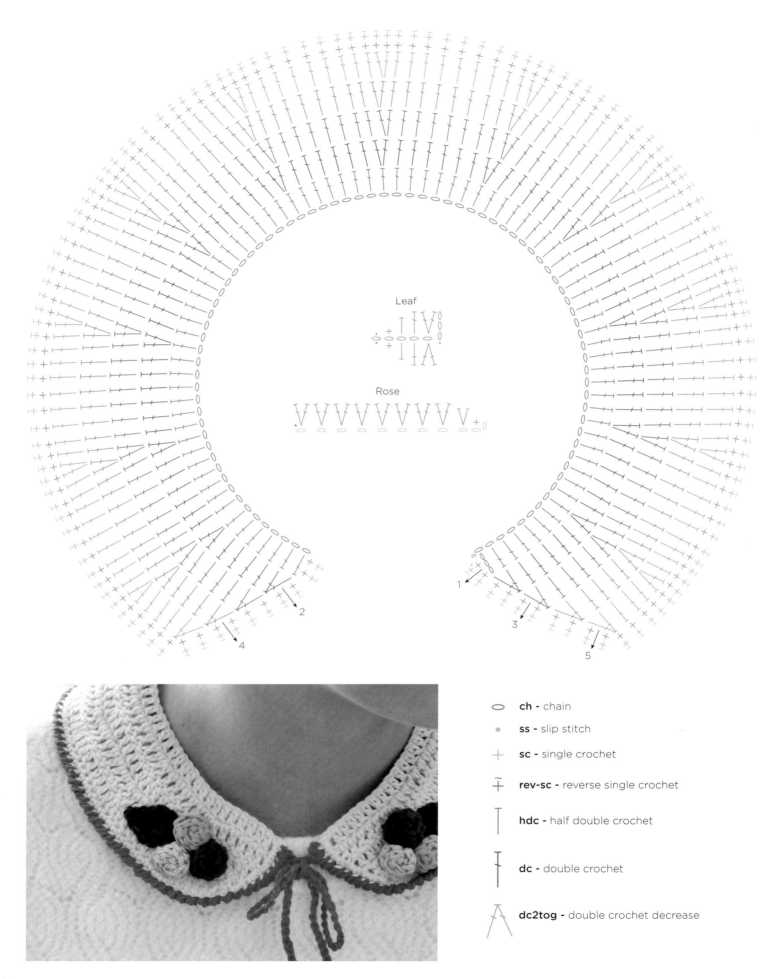

Leaf

Rose

ch - chain

ss - slip stitch

sc - single crochet

rev-sc - reverse single crochet

hdc - half double crochet

dc - double crochet

dc2tog - double crochet decrease

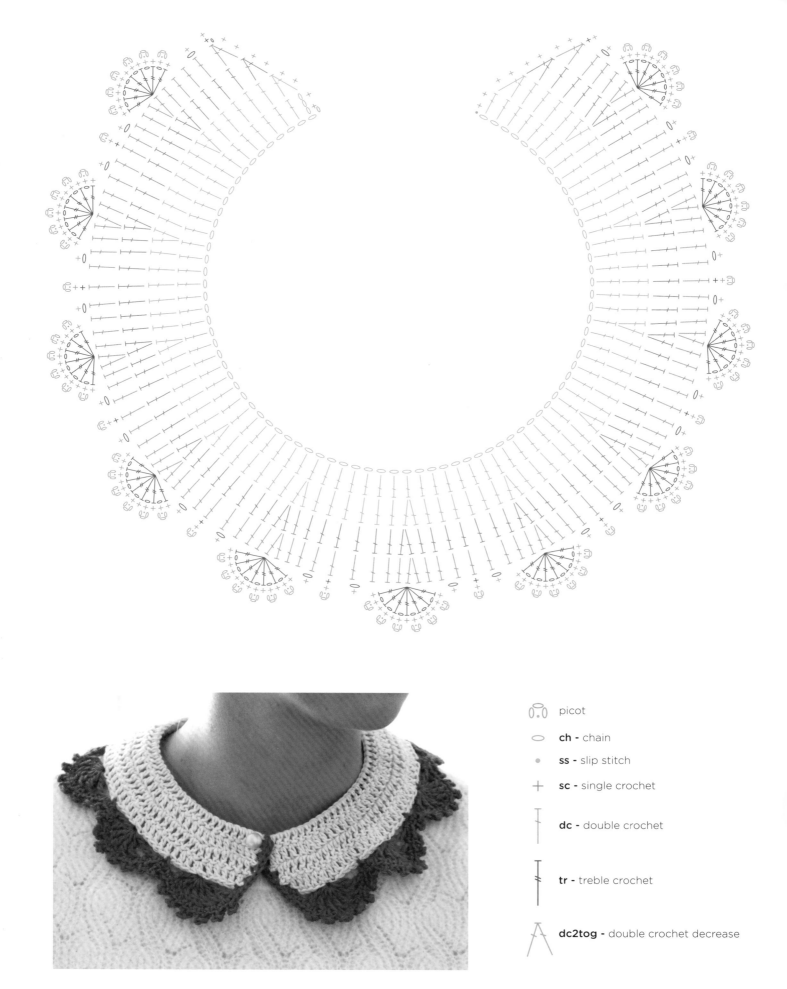

picot

ch - chain

ss - slip stitch

sc - single crochet

dc - double crochet

tr - treble crochet

dc2tog - double crochet decrease

Daisy Market Bag & Water Bottle Carriers

One of the most useful things I like to crochet are market bags. The Aran cotton used in this pattern makes this bag strong and durable while its solid base means your belongings will be safely stored. I've jazzed up a basic pattern with the addition of lots of crochet daisies - you could really go to town with them!

I've also created a matching water bottle carrier, perfect for when you want to travel light.

MARKET BAG

MATERIALS

Scheepjes Cahlista, 100% cotton, 50g/85m/93yds

Yarn A: Linen 505 x 6 balls
Yarn B: Primrose 522 x 1 ball
Yarn C: Snow White 106 x 1 ball

Blunt ended darning needle

Stitch Markers x 4

5mm (US8/H) and 5.5mm (US9/I) Crochet Hook

GAUGE

15 sts and 18 rows in single crochet to measure 4 x 4" (10 x 10cm) using 5mm (US8/H) hook and suggested yarn.

MEASUREMENTS

Market Bag Measures: approx. 14 x 16" (36 x 41cm) not including handles.

Handles Measure: approx. 27 x 1½" (68 x 4cm)

WATER BOTTLE CARRIERS

MATERIALS

Scheepjes Cahlista, 100% cotton, 50g/85m/93yds

Yarn A: Linen 505 x 2 balls (small 1 ball)
Yarn B: Primrose 522 x 1 ball
Yarn C: Snow White 106 x 1 ball

Blunt ended darning needle

Stitch Markers x 4

5mm (US8/H) and 5.5mm (US9/I) Crochet Hook

GAUGE

15 sts and 18 rows in single crochet to measure 4 x 4" (10 x 10cm) using 5mm (US8/H) hook and suggested yarn.

MEASUREMENTS

Large Carrier (to fit a 1L bottle) Measures: approx. 7 x 11" (18 x 28cm) circumference not including handles.

Handles Measure: approx. 27 x 1½" (68 x 4cm)

Small Carrier (to fit a 500ml bottle) Measures: approx. 6 x 7½" (15 x 19cm) circumference.

MARKET BAG

ABBREVIATIONS

Sp/s - space/s
Ch - chain
Sc – single crochet
Dc – double crochet
Ss – slip stitch
Rep – repeat
St/s – stitch/es
Sm – stitch marker

PATTERN NOTES

- Bag is worked in joined rounds, handles are worked as part of the bag and not added separately.

PATTERN STARTS

Rnd 1: Using 5mm (US8/H) hook and yarn A, ch54, 2sc in second ch from hook, 1sc in each of next 51 ch, 3sc in last ch, (now working into remaining loops of foundation chain), 1sc in each of next 51 ch, 1sc in last ch, join with ss to first st - 108sc.
Rnd 2: Ch1 (does not count as st here and throughout), 1sc in each st around, join with ss to first st.
Rnds 3-16: Rep rnd 2.
Rnd 17: Ch3 (counts as 1dc), 1dc in next st, ch1, skip 1 st, *1dc in each of next 2 sts, ch1, skip 1 st; rep from * around, join with ss to top of beginning ch 3.
Rnd 18: Ch1, 1sc in each st and ch1-sp around, join with a ss to first st - 108sc.
Rnd 19: Ch1, 1sc in each st around, join with ss to first st.
Rnd 20: Rep rnd 19.
Rnds 21-52: Rep rnds 17-20 eight more times.
Place a stitch marker in stitches 30, 54, 84 and 108 of rnd 52. These 4 markers will mark handle placement.
Rnd 53: Ch1, 1sc, *1sc in each st to sm (including marked stitch), ch100, skip 23 sts, 1sc in next marked st; (make sure chain is not twisted before re-joining to bag) rep from * once more, join with ss to first st of rnd.

Daisies (make 18)

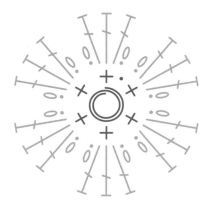

You should now have two 100ch handles attached to your bag.

Rnd 54: Ch1, 1sc in each st and ch around, join with ss to first st of rnd - 262sc.
Rnd 55: Ch1, 1sc in each st around, join with ss to first st of rnd.
Rnds 56–60: Rep rnd 55.
Rnd 61: Ss in each st around - 262ss.
Fasten off.

HANDLE EDGING

Rejoin yarn to inside of handles and ss in each st of inner handle and top edge of bag.
Rep for second handle. Fasten off, weave in ends.

DAISIES (MAKE 18)

Rnd 1: Using yarn B and 5.5mm (US9/I) hook, 6sc into magic ring, join with ss, switch to yarn C.
Rnd 2: Using 5mm (US8/H) hook, work (1ss, ch1, 3dc, ch1, 1ss) in each st around to create 6 petals, fasten off, weave in ends. Sew to bag using photo as a guide.

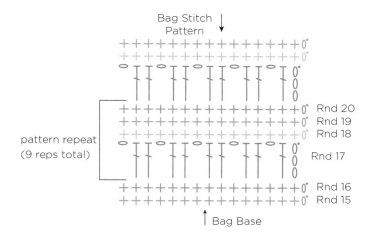

MR - magic ring + sc - single crochet

ch - chain dc - double crochet

ss - slip stitch

WATER BOTTLE CARRIERS

ABBREVIATIONS

Sp/s - space/s
Ch - chain
Sc – single crochet
Dc – double crochet
Ss – slip stitch
Rep – repeat
St/s – stitch/es

PATTERN NOTES

Water bottle carrier is worked in joined and un-joined rounds, handles are worked as part of the bag and not added separately.

PATTERN STARTS

LARGE WATER CARRIER (1 LITRE)

Use stitch marker to mark beginning of each rnd.

Rnd 1: Into magic ring, 6sc, do not join - 6sc.
Rnd 2: 2sc in each st around - 12sc.
Rnd 3: [1sc, 2sc in next st] around - 18sc.
Rnd 4: [2sc, 2sc in next st] around - 24sc.
Rnd 5: [3sc, 2sc in next st] around - 30sc.
Rnd 6: [4sc, 2sc in next st] around - 36sc.
Rnd 7: [5sc, 2sc in next st] around - 42sc.
Rnds 8-16: 1sc in each st around.
Rnd 17: 1sc in each st around, join with ss to first st of rnd.
Rnd 18: Ch3 (counts as 1dc), 1dc in next st, ch1, skip 1 st, *1dc in each of next 2 sts, ch1, skip 1 st; rep from * around, join with ss to top of beginning ch 3.
Rnd 19: Ch1 (does not count as st here and throughout), 1sc in each st and ch1-sp around, join with ss to first st - 42sc.
Rnd 20: Ch1, 1sc in each st around, join with ss to first st.
Rnd 21: Rep rnd 20.
Rnds 22-29: Rep rnds 18-21 twice more.
Rnd 30: Ch1, 1sc, ch100, skip 10 sts, 1sc in each of next 11 sts (make sure that chain is not twisted when re-joining to carrier), ch100, skip 10 sts, 1sc in each of next 10 sts, ss to first st of rnd.

You should now have two 100ch handles attached to your water bottle carrier.

Rnd 31: Ch1, 1sc in each st and ch around, join with ss to first st of rnd - 222sc.
Rnd 32: Ch1, 1sc in each st around, join with ss to first st of rnd.
Rnd 33: Rep rnd 32.
Rnd 34: Ss in each st around - 222ss.
Fasten off.

HANDLE EDGING

Rejoin yarn to inside of handles and ss in each st of inner handle and top edge of carrier.
Repeat for second handle. Fasten off, weave in ends.

DAISIES (MAKE 5)

Rnd 1: Using yarn B and 5.5mm (US9/I) hook, 6sc into magic ring, join with ss, switch to yarn C.
Rnd 2: Using 5mm (US8/H) hook, work (1ss, ch1, 3dc, ch1, 1ss) in each st around to create 6 petals, fasten off, weave in ends.

Sew to carrier using photo as a guide.

SMALL WATER CARRIER (500ML)

Use stitch marker to mark beginning of each rnd.

Rnds 1-5: Work as for Large Carrier - 30sc.
Rnds 6-12: 1sc in each st around.
Rnd 13: 1sc in each st around, join with ss to first st of rnd.
Rnd 14: Ch3 (counts as 1dc), 1dc in next st, ch1, skip 1 st, *1dc in each of next 2 sts, ch1, skip 1 st; rep from * around, join with ss to top of beginning ch 3.
Rnd 15: Ch1 (does not count as st here and throughout), 1sc in each st and ch1-sp around, join with ss to first st - 30sc.
Rnd 16: Ch1, 1sc in each st around, join with ss to first st.
Rnd 17: Rep rnd 16.
Rnds 18-25: Rep rnds 14-17 twice more.
Rnd 26: Ch1, 1sc, ch100, skip 7 sts, 1sc in each of next 8 sts (make sure that chain is not twisted when re-joining to carrier), ch100, skip 7 sts, 1sc in each of next 7 sts, ss to first st of rnd.
Rnd 27: Ch1, 1sc in each st and ch around, join with ss to first st of rnd.
Rnd 28: Ch1, 1sc in each st around, join with ss to first st of rnd.
Rnd 29: Rep rnd 28.
Rnd 30: Ss in each st around. Fasten off.

HANDLE EDGING

Rejoin yarn to inside of handles and ss in each st of inner handle and top edge of carrier.
Repeat for second handle. Fasten off, weave in ends.

Daisy

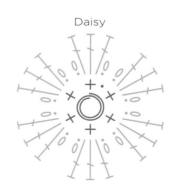

Base

Stitch Pattern

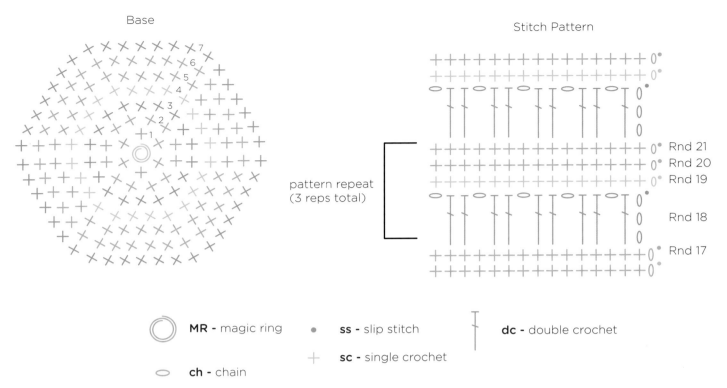

Rnd 21
Rnd 20
Rnd 19
Rnd 18
Rnd 17

pattern repeat
(3 reps total)

MR - magic ring   • **ss -** slip stitch   **dc -** double crochet

sc - single crochet

ch - chain

Drawstring Bag

Drawstring bags are so versatile. They can be used as evening bags or even to store your latest crochet project. I've designed this circular bag to have a solid base, so we're not going to lose those precious odds and ends we like to carry with us!

MATERIALS

Scheepjes Catona, 100% cotton mercerized, 50g/125m/137yds,

Shade: Rose Wine 396 x 2 balls

3.5mm/US4E Crochet Hook

Stitch Markers

Blunt Ended Darning Needle

Piece of Cardboard if desired cut to a circle with 6" (15cm) diameter.

GAUGE

Rnds 1 – 16 create a circle with an approx diameter of 6" (15cm) using suggested yarn and 3.5mm/US4E hook.

MEASUREMENTS

Finished Bag Measures: approx.
6" (15cm) diameter x 8½" (2cm) depth, 18½" (47cm) circumference.

ABBREVIATIONS

Sp/s - space/s
Ch - chain
Sc - single crochet
Dc - double crochet
Ss - slip stitch
Rep - repeat
St/s - stitch/es

SPECIAL STITCHES

Beg 3dc-cl

- Ch2 (counts as first half of first dc), *yarn over, insert hook into same st, yarn over, pull up a loop, yarn over, pull through 2 loops, (2 loops on hook); repeat from * once more (3 loops on hook), yarn over, pull through all 3 remaining loops.

3dc-cl

- *Yarn over, insert hook into st, yarn over, pull up a loop, yarn over, pull through 2 loops on hook (2 loops on hook); repeat from * twice more, (4 loops on hook), yarn over, pull through all 4 remaining loops.

PATTERN NOTES

- Base of bag is made in continuous rounds; use a stitch marker at the end of each round to keep track of your stitches. Lace pattern is then worked in joined rounds. If you'd like your bag to have a firm base, simply add a covered circle of cardboard to the inside of the bag.

PATTERN STARTS

BAG BASE

Insert stitch marker at the end of each round to keep track of stitches.

Make a magic ring

Rnd 1: 6sc into ring - 6sc.
Rnd 2: 2sc in each st around - 12sc.
Rnd 3: [1sc, 2sc in next st] around - 18sc.
Rnd 4: 1sc, 2sc in next st, [2sc, 2sc in next] to last st, 1sc in last st - 24sc.
Rnd 5: [3sc, 2sc in next st] around - 30sc.
Rnd 6: 2sc, 2sc in next st, [4sc, 2sc in next st] to last 2 sts, 2sc - 36sc.
Rnd 7: [5sc, 2sc in next st] around - 42sc.
Rnd 8: 3sc, 2sc in next st, [6sc, 2sc in next st] to last 3 sts, 3sc - 48sc.
Rnd 9: [7sc, 2sc in next st] around - 54sc.
Rnd 10: 4sc, 2sc in next st, [8sc, 2sc in next st] to last 4 sts, 4sc - 60sc.
Rnd 11: [9sc, 2sc in next st] around - 66sc.
Rnd 12: 5sc, 2sc in next st, *[10sc, 2sc in next st] to last 5 sts, 5sc - 72sc.

Rnd 13: [11sc, 2sc in next st] around - 78sc.
Rnd 14: 6sc, 2sc in next st, [12sc, 2sc in next st] to last 6 sts, 6sc - 84sc.
Rnd 15: [13sc, 2sc in next st] around - 90sc.
Rnd 16: 7sc, 2sc in next st, [14sc, 2sc in next st] to last 7 sts, 7sc - 96sc.
Rnd 17: 1sc in each st around.
Rnds 18-25: Rep rnd 17.
Rnd 26: Rep rnd 17, join with ss to beginning sc of rnd.

BAG BODY

Rnd 27: Ch1 (does not count as st), 1sc in first st, ch2, skip 2 sts, 1dc in next st, ch2, skip 2 sts, *1sc in next st, ch2, skip 2 sts, 1dc in next st, ch2, skip 2 sts; rep from * around, join with ss to beginning sc.
Rnd 28: Ch3 (counts as 1dc), skip 2 ch, (1cl, ch3, 1cl) in next dc, skip 2 ch, *1dc in next sc, skip 2 ch, (1cl, ch3, 1cl) in next dc, skip 2 ch; rep from * around, join with ss to top of beginning ch 3.
Rnd 29: Ch5 (counts as 1dc, 2ch), skip 1 cl, 1sc in ch3-sp, ch2, skip 1 cl, *1dc in next dc, ch2, skip 1 cl, 1sc in ch3-sp, ch2, skip 1 cl; rep from * around, join with ss to third ch of beginning ch 5.
Rnd 30: (Beg Cl, ch3, 1cl) in same st, skip 2 ch, 1dc in next sc, skip 2 ch, *(1cl, ch3, 1cl) in next dc, skip 2 ch, 1dc in next sc, skip 2 ch; rep from * around, join with ss to top of beg cl.
Rnd 31: Ss into next ch3-sp, ch1 (does not count as a st), 1sc in same ch3-sp, ch2, skip 1 cl, 1dc in next dc, ch2, skip 1 cl, *1sc in next ch3-sp, ch2, skip 1 cl, 1dc in next dc, ch2, skip 1 cl; rep from * around, join with a ss to beginning sc.
Rnd 32: Rep rnd 28.
Rnd 33: Rep rnd 29.
Rnd 34: Rep rnd 30.
Rnd 35: Rep rnd 31.
Rnd 36: Rep rnd 28.
Rnd 37: Rep rnd 29.
Rnd 38: Rep rnd 30.
Rnd 39: Rep rnd 31.
Rnd 40: Rep rnd 28.
Rnd 41: Rep rnd 29.
Rnd 42: Rep rnd 30.
Fasten off yarn, weave in ends.

TIES (MAKE 2)

Ch120. Fasten off (do not cut ends)

Using a darning needle thread one of the ties in and out of the stitches in rnd 39. Tie the ends. Repeat for the second tie but insert it on the opposite side of bag. Weave in ends.

If you would like your bag to have more structure, cut out a circle of cardboard to measure approx 15cm/6in in diameter, cover with fabric of choice and insert into base of bag.

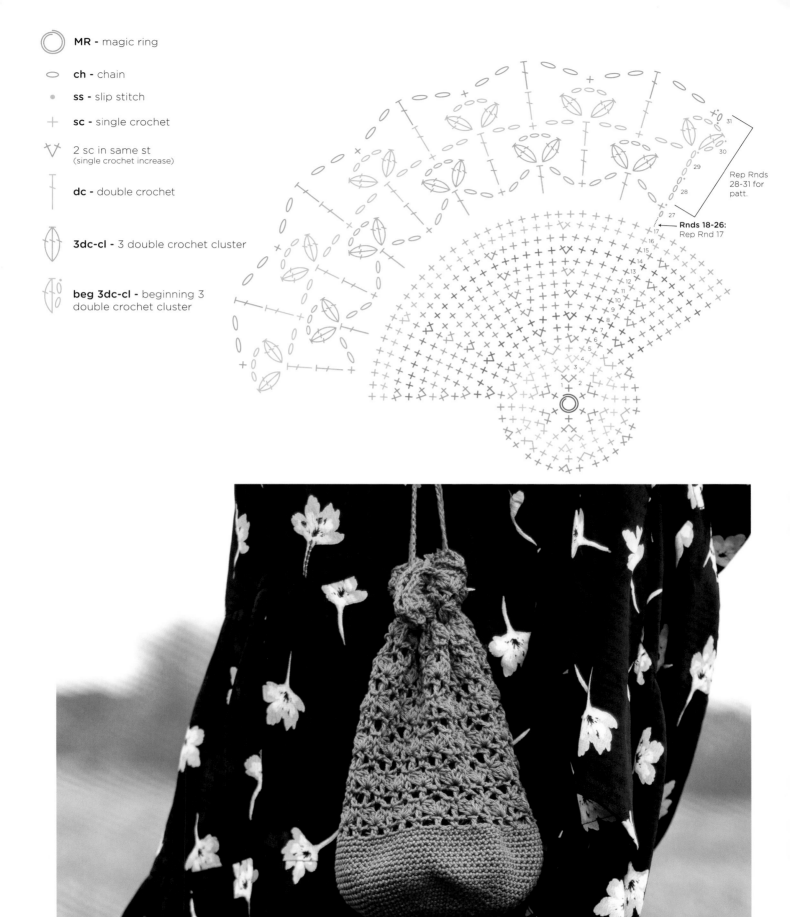

MR - magic ring

ch - chain

ss - slip stitch

sc - single crochet

2 sc in same st (single crochet increase)

dc - double crochet

3dc-cl - 3 double crochet cluster

beg 3dc-cl - beginning 3 double crochet cluster

Rep Rnds 28-31 for patt.

Rnds 18-26: Rep Rnd 17

Shawl

The colors from our walks in the New Forest have inspired this lacy shawl. Whenever I wear it I imagine myself as one of my favorite literary characters! Not only does it lend itself to daydreaming but, when worn as a scarf, it is incredibly practical for the reality of day to day life, including those chilly school runs.

MATERIALS

Scheepjes Stone Washed, 78% cotton, 22% acrylic, 50g/130m/142yds

Yarn A: Moonstone 801 x 2 balls
Yarn B: Axinite 831 x 1 ball
Yarn C: Enstatite 832 x 1 ball
Yarn D: Crystal Quartz 814 x 1 ball

5mm/H-8 crochet hook
Blunt ended darning needle

GAUGE

Pattern repeat is worked over 8 rows, from row 4-11.

18 sts and 9 rows in pattern to measure
5 x 5" (13 x 13cm) using 5mm/H-8 hook or size required to obtain gauge.

MEASUREMENTS

Finished Shawl (Before Blocking) Measures:

Width: 60" (152cm)

Depth (to point): 34" (86cm)

ABBREVIATIONS

Ch - chain
Sc - single crochet
Dc - double crochet
RS/WS - right side/wrong side
Rep - repeat
Sp/s - space/s
St/s - stitch/es
V-st - (1dc, ch3, 1dc) in next st

SPECIAL STITCHES

V-st

- (1dc, ch3, 1dc) in next st

PATTERN NOTES

- Ch 3 at start of row counts as 1dc. Final shawl does not need to be blocked, therefore blocking is optional.

TIPS

- Change to new shade of yarn on last pull through of last stitch of row of previous shade of yarn.

PATTERN STARTS

SHAWL

Row 1: With yarn A, ch5, join with a ss to form a ring, ch3 (counts as 1dc here and throughout) 4dc into ring, ch2, 5dc into ring, turn - 10 dc, 1 ch2-sp.

Row 2: Ch3, 2dc in same st, 1dc in each of next 4 sts, (2dc, ch2, 2dc) in ch2-sp, 1dc in each of next 4 sts, 3dc in last st, turn - 18 dc, 1 ch2-sp.

Row 3: Ch3, 2dc in same st, 1dc in each of next 8 sts, (2dc, ch2, 2dc) in ch2-sp, 1dc in each of next 8 sts, 3dc in last st, turn - 26 dc, 1 ch2-sp.

Switch to yarn B.

Row 4: Ch3, 2dc in same st, *skip 2 sts, V-st in next st, skip 2 sts, 1dc in next st; rep from * to center ch2-sp, (2dc, ch2, 2dc) in center ch2-sp, **1dc in next st, skip 2 sts, V-st in next st, skip 2 sts; rep from ** to last st, 3dc in last st, turn - 14dc, 4 v-sts, 1 ch2-sp.

Row 5: Ch3, 2dc in same st, *1ch, skip 3 sts, 5dc in next ch3-sp; rep from * to last ch3-sp before center ch2-sp, 1ch, skip 3 sts, 3dc in next st, (2dc, ch2, 2dc) in center ch2-sp, 3dc in next st, **1ch, skip 3 sts, 5dc in next ch3-sp; rep from ** to last ch3-sp of row, 1ch, skip 3 sts, 3dc in last st, turn - 36 dc, 6 ch1-sp, 1 ch2-sp.

Row 6: Ch3, 2dc in same st, *skip 2 sts, V-st in ch1-sp, skip 2 sts, 1dc in next st; rep from * to 2 sts before center ch2-sp, skip 2 sts, (2dc, ch2, 2dc) in center ch2-sp, **skip 2 sts, 1dc in next st, skip 2 sts, V-st in ch1-sp; rep from ** to last 3 sts, skip 2 sts, 3dc in last st, turn - 16 dc, 6 v-sts, 1 ch2-sp.

Row 7: Rep row 5 - 46 dc, 8 ch1-sp, 1 ch2-sp.
Switch to yarn A.
Row 8: Ch3, 2dc in same st, 1dc in every st and ch1-sp along to center sp, (2dc, ch2, 2dc) in center sp, 1dc in each st and ch1-sp to last st, 3dc in last st, turn - 62dc, 1 ch2-sp.
Row 9: Ch4 (counts as 1dc, ch1) 1dc in same st, *ch1, skip 1 st, 1dc in next st; rep from * to center ch2-sp, (ch1, 1dc, ch2, 1dc, ch1) into center sp, **1dc in next st, ch1, skip next st; rep from ** to last st, (1dc, ch1, 1dc) in last st, turn - 36 dc, 34 ch1-sp, 1 ch2-sp.
Switch to yarn C.
Row 10: Ch3, 2dc in same st, skip ch1 and 1dc, 1dc in next ch1-sp, 1dc into previous ch1-sp, *1dc in next unworked ch1-sp, working backwards across dc just made 1dc into previous ch1-sp (creating an x-st around each dc from row 9); rep from * to center sp working last rep into center ch2-sp, (2dc, ch2, 2dc) in center ch2-sp, 1dc in next unworked ch1-sp, 1dc back into center sp, **skip ch1 and 1dc, 1dc in next ch1-sp, 1dc into skipped ch1-sp; rep from ** along working 3dc in last st, turn - 78 dc (including 34 sets of crossed dc), 1 ch2-sp, 1 ch2-sp
Switch to yarn A.
Row 11: Ch3, 2dc in same st, 1dc in each st to center ch2-sp, (2dc, ch2, 2dc) in center ch2-sp, 1dc in each st to last st, 3dc in last st, turn - 86 dc, 1 ch2-sp.
Switch to yarn D.
Rows 12-19: Rep rows 4-11.
Switch to yarn B.
Rows 20-27: Rep rows 4-11.
Switch to yarn D.
Rows 28-35: Rep rows 4-11.

EDGING

Row 36: Rep row 4.
Switch to yarn C.
Row 37: Ch3, 2dc in same st, skip next st, 1sc in next st, *skip next st, 1dc in next ch3-sp, [1ch, 1dc] four times in same sp, skip next st, 1sc in next st; rep from * until 3rd st from center sp, 1dc in center sp, [1ch, 1dc] six times in same sp, skip 2 sts, 1sc in next st, **skip 1 st, 1dc in next ch3-sp, [1ch, 1dc] four times in same sp, skip next st, 1sc in next st; rep from ** to last 2 sts, skip next st, 3dc in last st.

FINISHING

Darn in loose ends.

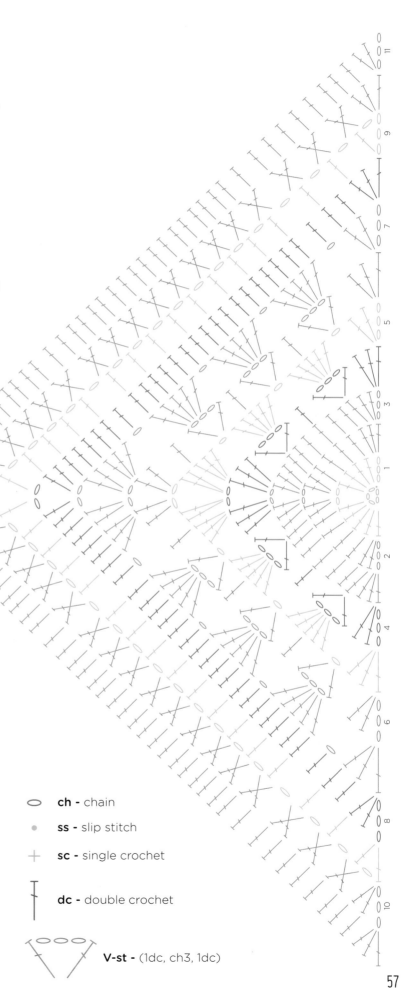

⬯ **ch -** chain

• **ss -** slip stitch

+ **sc -** single crochet

⊤ **dc -** double crochet

⬯⬯⬯ **V-st -** (1dc, ch3, 1dc)

Floral Face Cloth and Cleansing Pads

These reusable cotton floral face cloths and pads are simple to make. They can be popped in your washing machine and re-used, so are kinder to the environment and your wallet! I love to make a batch of these for gifts as they are pretty yet functional.

MATERIALS

Scheepjes Cahlista, 100% cotton, 50g/85m/93yds
Yarn A: Powder Pink 238 x 1 ball
Yarn B: Old Rose 408 x 1 ball
(1 ball of each is enough for 1 facecloth and 7 face pads)

5mm/US8-H Crochet Hook

Blunt Ended Darning Needle

Stitch Marker

GAUGE

Rounds 1 – 4 worked in single crochet measure a circle approx 2" (6cm) diameter using suggested yarn and 5mm/US8-H hook.

MEASUREMENTS

Finished Face Cloth Measures: approx. 10" (25cm) diameter (petal to petal),
Finished Face Pads Measure: approx. 3½" (9cm) diameter (petal to petal).

ABBREVIATIONS

Ch - chain
Sc - single crochet
Dc - double crochet
Tr - treble crochet
Ss - slip stitch
Rep - repeat
St/s - stitch/es

PATTERN NOTES

- Both face cloth and face pads are created using a basic circle pattern worked in continuous rounds, however, the increases are varied every other row to make a smoother finished circle.

PATTERN STARTS

FACE CLOTH

TIP: Place stitch marker at the end of each round to keep track of stitches.

Rnd 1: Using yarn A, 6sc into magic ring - 6sc.
Rnd 2: 2sc in each st around - 12sc.
Rnd 3: [1sc, 2sc in next st] around - 18sc.
Rnd 4: 1sc, 2sc in next st, [2sc, 2sc in next st] to last st, 1sc in last st - 24sc.
Rnd 5: [3sc, 2sc in next st] around - 30sc.

Rnd 6: 2sc, 2sc in next st, [4sc, 2sc in next st] to last 2 sts, 2sc - 36sc.
Rnd 7: [5sc, 2sc in next st] around - 42sc.
Rnd 8: 3sc, 2sc in next st, [6sc, 2sc in next st] to last 3 sts, 3sc - 48sc.
Rnd 9: [7sc, 2sc in next st] around - 54sc.
Rnd 10: 4sc, 2sc in next st, [8sc, 2sc in next st] to last 4 sts, 4sc - 60sc.
Rnd 11: [9sc, 2sc in next st] around - 66sc.
Rnd 12: 5sc, 2sc in next st, [10sc, 2sc in next st] to last 5 sts, 5sc - 72sc.
Rnd 13: [11sc, 2sc in next st] around - 78sc.
Rnd 14: 6sc, 2sc in next st, [12sc, 2sc in next st] to last 6 sts, 6sc - 84sc.
Rnd 15: [13sc, 2sc in next st] around, join with a ss - 90sc. Fasten off yarn A.
Rnd 16: Join yarn B to any st, 1sc in each st around, join with a ss.
Rnd 17: ch3 (counts as 1dc), 1dc in next st, 3tr in next st, 2dc, ss in next st, [2dc, 3tr in next st, 2dc, ss] around working last ss into ss from rnd 16.

FACE PADS

Rnds 1-4: Work as Facecloth.
Fasten off yarn A.

Rnd 5: Join yarn B to any st, ch1, *2dc in next st, 1dc, 2dc in next st, ss in next st; rep from * around working last ss into beginning ch 1. Fasten off yarn B, weave in ends.

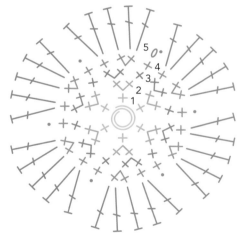

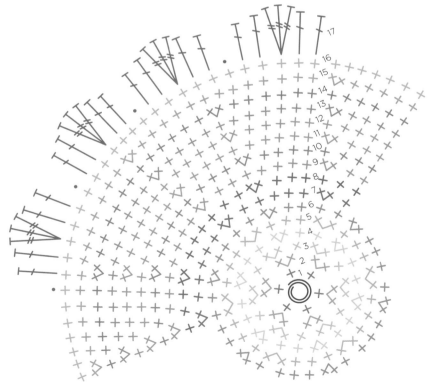

MR - magic ring

ch - chain

ss - slip stitch

sc - single crochet

2 single crochet in same st
(single crochet increase)

dc - double crochet

tr - treble crochet

Hand Towel and Cloth

I love versatile projects; this hand towel and cloth set are just that and would happily work well in the bathroom or kitchen. With the addition of another panel, the cloth can easily be adapted to create a potholder. I've used a pretty gingham style pattern with mini squares but feel free to experiment with your own color choices.

MATERIALS

Scheepjes Cahlista, 100% cotton, 50g/85m/93yds

Yarn A: Cherry 413 x 2 balls

Yarn B: Tulip 222 x 3 balls

Yarn C: Snow White 106 x 2 balls

Blunt ended darning needle

5mm (US8/H) crochet hook

GAUGE

One square worked in pattern measures 3" x 3" (7.5cm x 7.5cm) using 5mm hook and suggested yarn

MEASUREMENTS

Finished Hand Towel Measures: approx. 19" x 25" (48cm x 63.5cm)

Finished Cloth Measures: approx. 10" x 10" (25cm x 25cm)

ABBREVIATIONS

Ch - chain
Sc - single crochet
Dc - double crochet
Ss - slip stitch
Rep - repeat
St/s - stitch/es
RS/WS - right side/wrong side
Sp/s - space/s

PATTERN NOTES

- The first square is made whole, subsequent squares are then joined in the second round in rows. A total of 48 squares are worked for the hand towel and nine squares for the cloth. If you prefer to sew your squares together just make the required number of complete squares and sew together once finished.

- 'Joining square' refers to the square which is being joined to the square you are currently working.

PATTERN STARTS

HAND TOWEL

Row One - Square 1
With yarn A, create a magic ring.
Rnd 1: (RS) Ch3 (counts as 1dc here and throughout) 3dc in ring, ch2, [4dc in ring, ch2] three times, join with ss to beginning ch 3 - 16dc and four ch2-sp corners.
Rnd 2: (RS) Ch3, 1dc in each of next 3 sts, (2dc, ch2, 2dc) in corner ch2-sp, *4dc, (2dc, ch2, 2dc) in corner ch2-sp; rep from * twice more, join with ss to top of beginning ch 3 - 32dc, 4 x ch2-sp corners. Fasten off.

Row One - Square 2
Using photo as color guide, create magic ring.
Rnd 1: (RS) Work as rnd 1 of Square 1.
Rnd 2: (RS) Ch3, 3dc, (2dc, ch2, 2dc) in corner ch2-sp, *4dc, (2dc, ch1) in next corner ch2-sp, with RS of Square 1 facing, insert hook from front to back ss in ch2-sp of Square 1, 1dc in ch2-sp of Square 2, ss in next st of Square 1, 1dc in ch2-sp of Square 2, *ss in next st of Square 1, 1dc in next st of Square 2; rep from 3 more times, **ss in next st of Square 1, 1dc in corner ch2-sp of Square 2; rep from ** once more, ***ss in corner ch2-sp of Square 1 (join finished), ch1, 2dc in corner ch2-sp of Square 2, 1dc in each of next 4 sts, (2dc, ch2, 2dc) in last corner ch2-sp, join with ss to top of beginning ch 3.

Row One - Squares 3-6
Work as Square 2 joining to previous square as set.

Row Two - Square 1
Using photo as color guide, create magic ring.
Rnd 1: (RS) Ch3, 3dc in loop, ch2, [4dc in ring, ch2] three times, join with ss to beginning ch 3 - 16dc.

Rnd 2: Joining to square 1 in row 1, work as squares 2-6 as above, but on last joining ss (marked ***), work ss in corner ch2-sp of square 2 below (diagonally – this will remove the gaps as you join corner to corner).

Row Two - Squares 2 To 6.
Using photo as color guide, create magic ring.
Rnd 1: (RS) Ch3, 3dc in ring, ch2, [4dc in ring, ch2] three times, join with ss to beginning ch 3 - 16dc.
Rnd 2: Working the joins in same way as on row 1, join squares to each other along two sides (to both the square directly below and to the previous square). Where corners meet, be sure to work the ss diagonally into the corner of the row below then continue to join the upper and lower squares together (see diagram).

Rows Three To Eight
Repeat Row 2.
You should now have a hand towel with 48 joined squares

TOWEL EDGING

With RS facing join yarn C to corner ch2-sp at top of one long edge.
Rnd 1: *79sc evenly along to corner ch2-sp, 3sc in corner ch2-sp, 61sc along short edge to next ch2-sp, 3sc in corner ch2-sp; rep from * once more, join with a ss. Fasten off yarn A.
Rnd 2: Join yarn B to corner st, ch3 (counts as 1dc), 4dc in same st, skip 1 st, 1sc in next st, *skip 2 sts, 5dc in next st, skip 2 sts, 1sc in next st; rep from * to next corner, skip 1 corner st, 5dc in next corner st, skip next corner st, 1sc in next st**; rep from * to ** three more times, ending last rep with a ss to top of beginning ch 3. Fasten off.

FACE CLOTH

Working as towel, make a cloth of 3 x 3 squares using photo as color guide.

FACE CLOTH EDGING

Rnd 1: Using yarn A work 31sc evenly along each side of cloth and 3sc in each corner ch2-sp.
Rnd 2: Work as for rnd 2 of Towel Edging. Fasten off.

TO FINISH

Weave in ends.

S2/R2   S1/R2

MR - magic ring

ch - chain

ss - slip stitch

sc - single crochet

dc - double crochet

S3/R1   S2/R1   S1/R1

Hot Water Bottle Cosy

There is something so comforting about a hot water bottle, whether it's used to warm you or to comfort aches and pains. This hot water bottle cosy has been created in the most beautiful Merino mix yarn which together with those tactile bobble stitches makes it perfect to cozy up to.

MATERIALS

Scheepjes Merino Soft Brush,
50% superwash Merino, 25% micro, 25% acrylic, 50g/105m/115yds,

Shade: Van Dyck 256 x 3 balls

Blunt ended darning needle

4.5mm/US7 crochet hook

GAUGE

17 sts and 22 rows over single crochet to measure 4" x 4" (10 x 10cm) using suggested yarn and 4.5mm/7 crochet hook or size required to obtain gauge.

MEASUREMENTS

Hot Water Bottle Cosy Measures: approx. 8" x 10½" (20 x 27cm) across widest part, and not including length of neck.

To fit a standard 2 litre flashy hot water bottle.

ABBREVIATIONS

Ch - chain
Sc - single crochet
Dc - double crochet
Fpdc - front post double crochet
Bpdc - back post double crochet
Ss - slip stitch
Rep - repeat
St/s - stitch/es

SPECIAL STITCHES

Bobble

– *Yarn over, insert hook into stitch to be worked, yarn over, pull through a loop, yarn over, pull through 2 loops on hook; repeat from * four more times (6 loops on the hook), yarn over, pull through all 6 loops, ch1 to close.

PATTERN NOTES

- The hot water bottle cosy is worked in two pieces, which are then joined leaving a neck opening. The neck of the hot water cosy is then worked in rounds onto the opening. Bobbles will appear on the right side of the work as you work them on the wrong side. The closing ch1 of each bobble does not count as a stitch. Make sure your hot water bottle is empty before you insert or remove it from the cover.

PATTERN STARTS

FRONT AND BACK (BOTH ALIKE)

Row 1: Ch26, 1sc in second ch from hook, 1sc in each of next 24ch, turn - 25sc.
Row 2: Ch1 (does not count as st here and throughout), 2sc in same st, 1sc in each of next 23 sts, 2sc in last st, turn - 27sc.
Row 3: Ch1, 2sc in same st, 3sc, [bobble in next st, 5sc] three times, bobble in next st, 3sc, 2sc in last st, turn - 29 sts.
Row 4: Ch1, 2sc in same st, 1sc in each of next 27 sts, 2sc in last st, turn - 31 sts.
Row 5: Ch1, 2sc in same st, 4sc, [bobble in next st, 1sc, bobble in next st, 3sc] four times to last 2 sts, 1sc, 2sc in last st, turn - 33 sts.
Row 6: Ch1, 1sc in same st, 1sc in each st along, turn.
Row 7: Ch1, 7sc, [bobble in next st, 5sc] four times to last 2 sts, 2sc, turn.
Rows 8 - 10: Rep row 6.
Row 11: Ch1, 4sc, [bobble in next st, 5sc] four times, bobble in next st, 4sc, turn.
Row 12: Rep row 6.
Row 13: Ch1, 3sc, [bobble in next st, 1sc, bobble in next st, 3sc] five times, turn.
Row 14: Rep row 6.

Row 15: Rep row 11.
Rows 16 - 18: Rep row 6.
Row 19: Rep row 7.
Row 20: Rep row 6.
Row 21: Ch1, 6sc, [bobble in next st, 1sc, bobble in next st, 3sc] four times to last 3 sts, 3sc, turn.
Row 22: Rep row 6.
Row 23: Rep row 7.
Rows 24 - 39: Rep rows 8 - 23.
Rows 40 - 52: Rep rows 8 - 20.
Row 53: Skip first st (decrease made), 5sc, [bobble in next st, 1sc, bobble in next st, 3sc] four times, 2sc, skip last st (decrease made), turn - 31 sts.
Row 54: Skip first st (decrease made), 29sc, skip last st (decrease made), turn - 29 sts.
Row 55: Skip first st (decrease made), 4sc, [bobble in next st, 5sc] three times, bobble in next st, 4sc, skip last st (decrease made), turn - 27 sts.
Row 56: Skip first st (decrease made), 25sc, skip last st (decrease made), turn - 25 sts.
Row 57: Skip first st (decrease made), 23sc, skip last st (decrease made), turn - 23 sts.
Row 58: Skip first st (decrease made), 21sc, skip last st (decrease made), turn - 21 sts.
Row 59: Skip first st (decrease made), 19sc, skip last st (decrease made) - 19 sts.
Fasten off and weave in ends.

JOINING

With bobbles facing outwards join sides from top edge of neck opening by working 1sc into side of each row, 3sc into the corner, 1sc into each remaining chain loop of foundation row, 3sc into next corner and 1sc into side of each row up to the neck opening.

NECK OPENING

Rnd 1: Work 38sc evenly around neck opening and join with a ss.
Rnd 2: Ch3 (counts as 1dc), 1dc in each st around, join with a ss to top of beginning ch 3 - 38 sts.
Rnd 3: Ch3 (counts as 1dc), [1fpdc in next st, 1bpdc in next st] around, join with a ss to top of beginning ch 3.
Rnds 4 - 13: Rep rnd 3 or until neck measures approx 4" (10cm) and can easily be turned in half.
Fasten off, weave in ends.

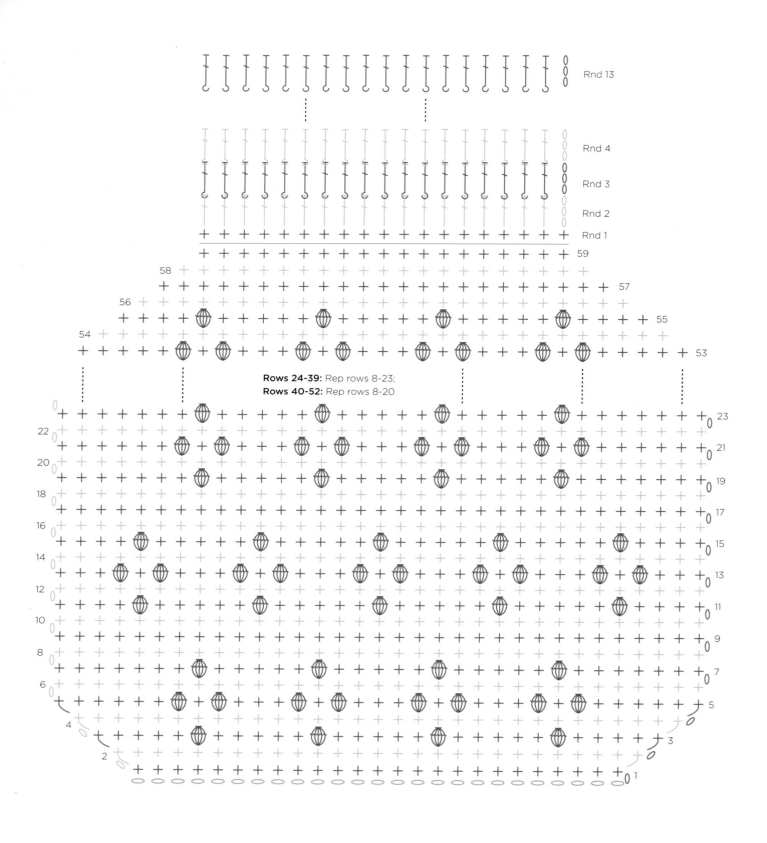

Rows 24-39: Rep rows 8-23;
Rows 40-52: Rep rows 8-20

ch - chain

ss - slip stitch

sc - single crochet

dc - double crochet

fpdc - front post double crochet

bpdc - back post double crochet

5-dc-bobble

Lacy Cocoon Shrug

This light and lacy cotton shrug is a perfect project for the warmer months. Using a beautiful fan stitch pattern, it's made from one rectangle of crochet making it deceptively simple.

MATERIALS

Scheepjes Catona, 100% mercerized cotton, 50g/125m/137yds

Shade: Old Lace 130 x 5 balls

4.5mm/US7 crochet hook

Blunt ended darning needle

GAUGE

Work 12 sts (2 patt reps) to 5½" (14cm) and 9 rows to 4⅔" (12cm) using 4.5mm hook, measured before blocking.

MEASUREMENTS

Finished Shrug Measures: approx. 39" (100cm) from cuff to cuff x 33½" (85cm) from top to bottom after blocking.

ABBREVIATIONS

Ch - chain
Sc – single crochet
Dc – double crochet
Ss – slip stitch
Rep – repeat
St/s – stitch/es
Sp/s – space/s

PATTERN NOTES

- Cocoon shrug is made of one rectangular piece of crochet, which is then folded in half and seamed along the short edges, leaving gaps for armholes. This is a one size garment however, if you wish to make your shrug longer just continue to repeat rows 2-4 until you reach the desired length. To adjust width add or remove pattern repeats to starting chain in multiples of 12 sts.

PATTERN STARTS

With 4.5mm/US7 hook, ch156.

Row 1: Ch5 (counts as 1dc, 2ch), 1sc in 7th ch from hook, ch2, skip 3 ch, 5dc in next ch, ch2, skip 3 ch, 1sc in next ch, *ch5, skip 3 ch, 1sc in next ch, ch2, skip 3 ch, 5dc in next ch, ch2, skip 3 ch, 1sc in next ch; rep from * to last 2 ch, ch2, skip 1 ch, 1dc in last ch, turn.

Row 2: Ch1 (does not count as st), 1sc in same st, ch2, skip next two ch2-sps, *(1dc, 1ch) in each of next 4 dc, 1dc in next dc, ch2, skip next ch2-sp and sc,** 1sc in next ch5-sp, ch2, skip next ch2-sp and sc; rep from * along ending last rep at **, skip 2 ch, 1sc in 3rd ch of ch 5 (turning chain), turn.

Row 3: Ch3 (counts as 1dc), *skip next ch2-sp, (1dc, ch2) in each of next 4 dc, 1dc in next dc, skip next ch2-sp and sc; rep from * along, ending with 1dc in last sc of row, turn.

Row 4: Ch5 (counts as 1dc, 2ch), skip 1 dc, 1sc in next ch2-sp, ch2, skip next dc and ch2-sp, 5dc in next dc, ch2, skip next ch2-sp and dc, * 1sc in next ch2-sp, ch5, 1sc in next ch2-sp, ch2, skip next dc and ch2-sp, 5dc in next dc, ch2, skip next ch2-sp and dc; rep from * along, 1sc in last ch-2sp, ch2, 1dc in 3rd of ch 3.

Rows 2 to 4 form pattern and are repeated.
Work a further 17 pattern repeats.
Work rows 2 and 3 once more.
Fasten off.

TO MAKE UP

Block work to measure 39″ (100cm) x 33½″ (85cm). Fold piece in half lengthways (so that first and final rows are touching). Seam up the sides using a whip stitch, leaving approx 7″ (18cm) from fold line for armholes – see diagram.

ARMBANDS

Rnd 1: Work 50sc evenly around armhole opening, join with ss.
Rnd 2: 1sc in each sc around, join with ss.
Fasten off.

TO FINISH

Weave in ends. To make the most of the scalloped edging around the neckline, wear your shrug with fans facing upwards.

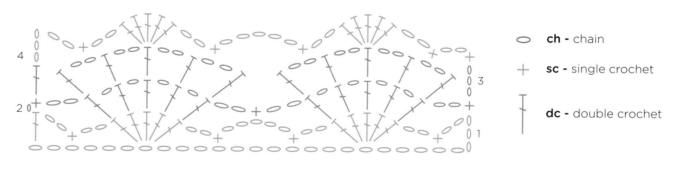

4 / 2 / 3 / 1

○ **ch -** chain

+ **sc -** single crochet

T **dc -** double crochet

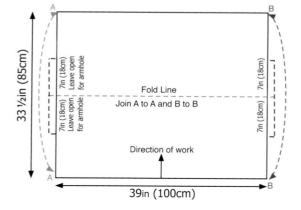

A / B / 33 ½in (85cm) / 7in (18cm) Leave open for armhole / 7in (18cm) Leave open for armhole / Fold Line / Join A to A and B to B / 7in (18cm) / 7in (18cm) / Direction of work / A / B / 39in (100cm)

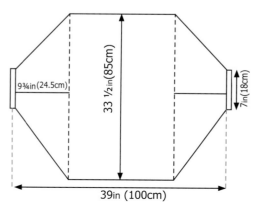

9¾in (24.5cm) / 33 ½in(85cm) / 7in(18cm) / 39in (100cm)

Lacy Short Sleeved Top

I'm always drawn to cotton crochet tops when the weather starts to warm, they remind me of warm, hazy, dreamy summer days, even if the reality is a great British Summer. This top is so simple in its construction, made from two panels - it's all about the stitch pattern. The picot edging on the sleeves and bottom of the top add a sweet finish.

MATERIALS

Scheepjes Soft Fun, 60% cotton, 40% acrylic, 50g/140m/153yds

Shade: Snow White 2412 x 4 (5, 7) balls

Blunt ended darning needle

4mm/US6-G crochet hook

4 x Stitch markers

GAUGE

2 stitch pattern repeats (24 sts) x 2 row repeats (12 rows) to 6¼"x 6" (16 x 15cm) square worked in pattern using 4mm/US6-G hook and suggested yarn - after blocking

MEASUREMENTS

To Fit	Finished Bust		Finished Length	
	cm	inch	cm	inch
Small	96	38	48	19
Medium	112	44	52	20½
Large	128	50½	55	21⅔

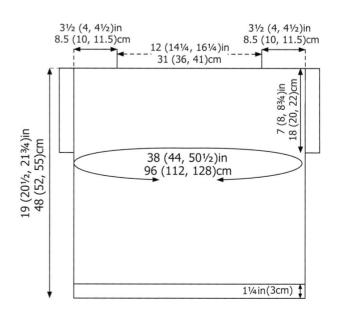

ABBREVIATIONS

Ch - chain
Sc – single crochet
Dc – double crochet
Tr – treble crochet
Ss – slip stitch
Rep – repeat
St/s – stitch/es
Sp/s - space/s
RS/WS - right side/wrong side

SPECIAL STITCHES

Picot

- Ch3, ss into sc directly below.

PATTERN NOTES

- Top is created by working two panels (front and back), which are then joined along the sides and the shoulders, leaving gaps for arm holes. Small sleeve details are then worked in the round around the armholes, the same edging is worked around the bottom of the T-shirt.
  This pattern can be adapted for any size by adjusting your starting chain in multiples of 12.

PATTERN STARTS

BACK AND FRONT (BOTH ALIKE)

Row 1: Ch76 (88, 100) (counts as 73 (85, 97)ch + 1dc), 1dc in fifth ch from hook, *ch3, skip 3 ch, 1sc in next ch, ch2, skip 1 ch, 1sc in next ch, ch3, skip 3 ch, 1dc in each of next 3 sts; rep from * 4 (5, 6) more times to last 11 ch, ch3, skip 3 ch, 1sc in next ch, ch2, skip 1 ch, 1sc in next ch, ch3, skip 3 ch, 1dc in each of last 2 sts. Turn.

Row 2: Ch3 (counts as 1dc here and throughout), 1dc in next st, *2dc in ch3-sp, ch3, skip 1sc, 1sc in ch2-sp, ch3, 2dc in next ch3-sp, 1dc in each of next 3 sts; rep from * along to last rep, 2dc in ch3-sp, ch3, skip 1sc, 1sc in last ch2-sp, ch3, 2dc in last ch3-sp, 1dc in each of last 2 sts. Turn.

Row 3: Ch3, 1dc in each of next 3 sts, *2dc in ch3-sp, ch2, skip 1sc, 2dc in next ch3-sp, 1dc in each of next 7 sts; rep from * along to last rep, 2dc in ch3-sp, ch2, skip 1sc, 2dc in last ch3-sp, 1dc in each of last 4 sts. Turn.

Row 4: Ch1 (does not count as st), 2sc, *ch3, skip 4 sts, 3dc in next ch2-sp, ch3, miss 4 sts, 1sc in next st, ch2, skip 1 st, 1sc in next st; rep from * along to last rep, ch3, skip 4 sts, 3dc in last ch2-sp, ch3, skip 4 sts, 1sc in each of last 2 sts. Turn.

Row 5: Ch1 (doesn't count), 1sc, *ch3, skip 1sc, 2dc in next ch3-sp, 1dc in each of next 3 sts, 2dc in next ch3-sp, ch3, skip 1sc, 1sc in ch2-sp; rep from * to last repeat, ch3, 2dc in ch3-sp, 1dc in each of next 3 sts, 2dc in last ch3-sp, ch3, skip 1sc, 1sc in last st. Turn.

Row 6: Ch5 (counts as 1tr, ch1), *2dc in next ch3-sp, 1dc in each of next 7 sts, 2dc in next ch3-sp, ch2 skip 1sc; rep from * along to last repeat, 2dc in next ch3-sp, 1dc in each of next 7 sts, 2dc in last ch3-sp, ch1, 1tr in last st. Turn.

Row 7: Ch3, 1dc in ch1-sp, *ch3, skip 4 sts, 1sc in next st, ch2, skip 1 st, 1sc in next st, ch3, skip 4 sts, 3dc in ch2-sp; rep from along to last repeat, ch3, skip 4 sts, 1sc in next st, ch2, skip 1 st, 1sc in next st, ch3, skip 4 sts, 1dc in ch1-sp, 1dc in fourth ch of turning ch. Turn.

Row 8: Repeat row 2.
Row 9: Repeat row 3.
Row 10: Repeat row 4.
Row 11: Repeat row 5.
Row 12: Repeat row 6.
Row 13: Repeat row 7.
Row 14: Repeat row 2.
Row 15: Repeat row 3.
Row 16: Repeat row 4.
Row 17: Repeat row 5.
Row 18: Repeat row 6.
Row 19: Repeat row 7.
Row 20: Repeat row 2.
Row 21: Repeat row 3.
Row 22: Repeat row 4.
Row 23: Repeat row 5.
Row 24: Repeat row 6.
Row 25: Repeat row 7.
Row 26: Repeat row 2.
Row 27: Repeat row 3.
Row 28: Repeat row 4.
Row 29: Repeat row 5.
Row 30: Repeat row 6.
Row 31: Repeat row 7.
Row 32: Repeat row 2.
Row 33: Repeat row 3.
Row 34: Repeat row 4.
Row 35: Repeat row 5.
Row 36: Repeat row 6.

Sizes M and L only
Row 37: Repeat row 7.
Row 38: Repeat row 2.
Row 39: Repeat row 3.

Size L only
Row 40: Repeat row 4.
Row 41: Repeat row 5.
Row 42: Repeat row 6.

All Sizes fasten off.

EDGING

You will now be working into the remaining loops of your foundation chain.

Row 1: With RS facing rejoin yarn to first remaining loop of foundation chain. Work 1sc in each ch along, turn - 73 (85, 97) sc.

Row 2: Ch4 (counts as 1dc, ch1), skip 1 st, *1dc in next st, ch1, skip 1st; rep * along, ending with 1dc in last st. Turn.

Row 3: Ch1 (does not count as st), 1sc, * (1sc, picot) in ch1-sp, 1sc in next st; rep along. Fasten off.

TO JOIN

With both pieces together, place stitch markers on each side, approx 7" (8", 8⅔"), (18 (20, 22)cm) down from shoulder for armholes. Sew sides together from bottom up using a whip stitch (or preferred seaming method) leaving armholes open.

Along top measure 3½" (4", 4½"), (8.5 (10, 11.5)cm) from each outer edge, and place a stitch marker at both points (neck opening will measure 12" (14¼", 16¼"), (31 (36, 41)cm). Join shoulders from armholes to stitch markers using same method as side seams.

ARM BANDS

Rnd 1: Rejoin yarn to armhole opening, Work 61 (67, 75) sc evenly around opening, join with ss to first sc.
Rnd 2: Ch4 (counts as 1dc, ch1), skip 1 st, *1dc in next st, ch1, skip 1st; rep * along, join with ss to ch3 of beginning ch 4.
Rnd 3: Ch1 (does not count as a st), 1sc, *(1sc, picot) in ch1-sp, 1sc in next st; rep along, join with ss to first sc. Fasten off.

TO FINISH

Weave in ends.

Pattern repeat rows 2 - 7

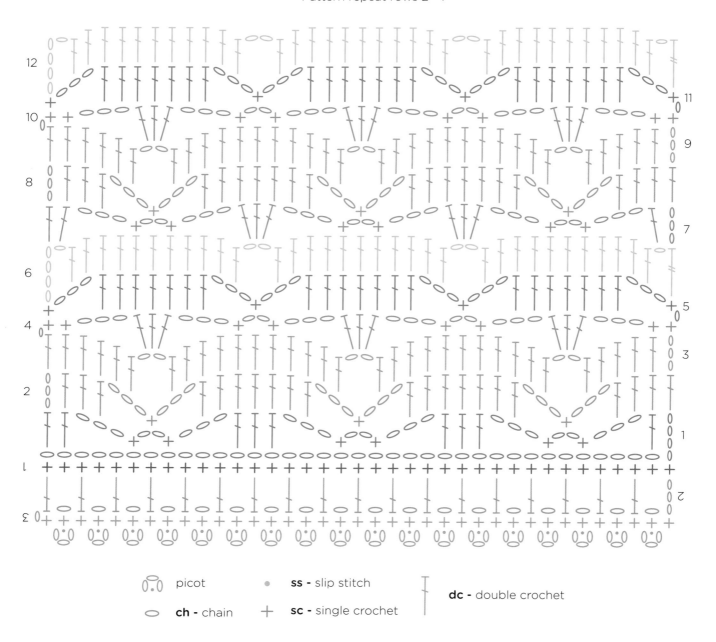

picot	**ss -** slip stitch	**dc -** double crochet
ch - chain	**sc -** single crochet	

Rambling Rose Cushion

This cushion was inspired by the delicate rambling roses of summer. I wanted to create a picture of those roses that I could enjoy all year; so I crocheted one. It requires some simple colorwork to create a window frame effect. The bobble stitches and roses give this cushion a fabulous texture that, combined with the beautiful stone washed yarn, make the picture come to life.

MATERIALS

Scheepjes Stonewashed XL, 70% cotton, 30% acrylic, 50g/75m/82yds

Yarn A: Moonstone 841 x 5 ball

Yarn B: Brown Agate 862 x 1 ball

Yarn C: Crystal Quartz 854 x 2 balls

Yarn D: Rose Quartz 860 x 1 ball

Yarn E: Rhodochrosite 875 x 1 ball

Yarn F: Canada Jade 846 x 1 ball

5mm/US8-H crochet hook

Blunt ended darning needle

Needle and white sewing thread

GAUGE

13 sts and 14 rows in single crochet to measure 4" x 4" (10 x 10cm) using 5mm/US8-H hook and suggested yarn.

MEASUREMENTS

Finished Cushion Panel Measures: approx. 16½" (42cm) square.

Designed to fit a standard 16" (40cm) square cushion pad.

ABBREVIATIONS

Ch - chain
Sc – single crochet
Dc - double crochet
Hdc - half double crochet
Ss – slip stitch
Rep – repeat
St/s – stitch/es
Sp/s - space/s
RS/WS - right side/wrong side

SPECIAL STICHES

Bobble Stitch

- *Yarn over hook, insert hook into st to be worked, yarn over hook, pull up a loop (3 loops on hook), yarn over hook, pull through 2 loops; rep from * four more times (6 loops on hook), yarn over and pull through all loops, ch1 to close st (ch1 does not count as a separate st).

V-St

- (1dc, ch1, 1dc) into same st.

PATTERN NOTES

- Bobble stitches are worked on WS rows (bobbles will appear on the RS).
- When working color changes along the rows after row 7, carry yarn not in use along back of work and crochet over the yarn to hide it, as for tapestry crochet.
- When changing colors, change on last st before the color change by working last pull through of last st in new yarn then drop the old color.
- When changing colors after a bobble st, work bobble stitch in old color and pull the new shade through in the closing ch1.

PATTERN STARTS

FRONT PANEL

Row 1: (RS) Using yarn A, ch54, 1sc in second ch from hook, 1sc in each ch to end, turn - 53sc.
Row 2: (WS) Ch1 (does not count as st here and throughout), 1sc in each st to end, turn - 53sc.
Rows 3-7: Rep row 2.
Row 8: Ch1, 7sc, switch to yarn B, [1 bobble in next st, 1sc] 19 times, 1 bobble in next st, switch to yarn A, 7sc, turn - 20 bobble sts, 33sc.
Row 9: Ch1, 7sc, switch to yarn B, 1sc in bobble st, switch to yarn C, 1sc, [1sc in bobble, 1sc] 18 times, switch to yarn B, 1sc in bobble, switch to yarn A, 7sc, turn - 53sc.
Row 10: Ch1, 7sc, switch to yarn B, 1 bobble in next st, switch to yarn C, 37sc, switch to yarn B, 1 bobble in next

st, switch to yarn A, 7sc, turn - 2 bobble sts, 51sc.
Row 11: Ch1, 7sc, switch to yarn B, 1sc in bobble, switch to yarn C, 37sc, switch to yarn B, 1sc in bobble, switch to yarn A, 7sc, turn - 53sc
Rows 12-47: Rep rows 10 and 11 (18 times).
Row 48: Rep row 8.
Rows 49-55: Rep row 2.
Fasten off yarn, weave in ends.

LARGE ROSES (MAKE 2)

Row 1: (WS) Using yarn D, ch36, 1sc in second ch from hook, skip 1 ch, [V-st in next ch, skip 1 ch] to last st, 1dc in last st, turn - 16 V-sts.
Row 2: (RS) Ch1 (does not count as st) 1sc, *5dc in centre of next V-st, 1sc in sp before next V-st; rep from * 13 more times, 5hdc in centre of next V-st, ss in sp before next V-st, 5hdc in centre of next V-st, ss in last st. Fasten off yarn D leaving approx 8" (20cm) tail for sewing up rose.
Row 3: With RS facing switch to yarn E, ch2, skip first st, *1sc in each of next 2 sts, 2sc in next st, 1sc in each of next 2 sts, 1sc (working over sc from row 2 and into sp between V-sts in row 1); rep from * to last st, ss into last st. Fasten off.

Create rose by curling piece around itself and sewing up as you go (making sure shorter stitches from row 2 are at the center).

SMALL ROSES (MAKE 3)

Row 1: Using yarn D, ch18, 1sc in second ch from hook, skip 1 ch, [V-st in next ch, skip 1 ch] to last st, 1dc in last st, turn - 16 V-sts
Row 2: Ch1 (doesn't count as st) 1sc, *5dc in center of next V-st, 1sc in sp before next V-st; rep from * four more times, 5hdc in centre of next V-st, ss in sp before next V-st, 5hdc in centre of next V-st, ss in last st.

Fasten off leaving approx 8" (20cm) tail for sewing up rose. Sew up as for Large Rose.

LEAVES (MAKE 5)

Using yarn F, ch10, 3dc in fourth ch from hook, 1dc in each of next 3 ch, 1hdc in next ch, 1sc in next ch, ss into next ch, ch1 (you will now be working into remaining loops of chain), ss in next ch, 1sc in next ch, 1hdc in next ch, 1dc in each of next next 3 ch, 3dc in last ch, join with ss. Fasten off weave in ends.

Sew leaves and roses to front of cushion panel, with sewing thread, using photo as a guide.

BACK PANELS

If your tapestry crochet has increased the tension in your row height you may want to go up half a hook size for back panels.

TOP PANEL

Row 1: Using yarn A, ch54, 1sc into second ch from hook, 1sc in each ch to end, turn - 53sc.
Row 2: Ch1 (does not count as st here and throughout), 1sc in each st to end, turn - 53sc.
Rows 3-29: Rep row 2.
Row 30: Ch1, 1sc in same st, *9sc, ch1, skip 1, 1sc in next st (button hole made); rep from * once more, 8sc, ch1, skip 1, 1sc in next st (button hole made), 9sc, ch1, skip 1, 1sc in next st (button hole made), 9sc, turn - 49sc, 4 ch1-sps.
Row 31: Ch1, 1sc in each st and ch1-sp to end - 53sc.
Fasten off.

BOTTOM PANEL

Row 1: Using yarn A, ch54, 1sc in second ch from hook, 1sc in each ch to end, turn - 53sc.
Row 2: Ch1 (does not count as st here and throughout), 1sc in each st to end, turn - 53sc.
Rows 3-31: Rep row 2.
Fasten off.

TO FINISH

With WS's facing, pin both Back Panels to Front Panel (there should be an overlap of 7 rows on back panels). Working on front side of cushion and through front and back panels work 1sc in each st and row around entire cushion working 3sc into each corner space. Fasten off. Weave in ends.

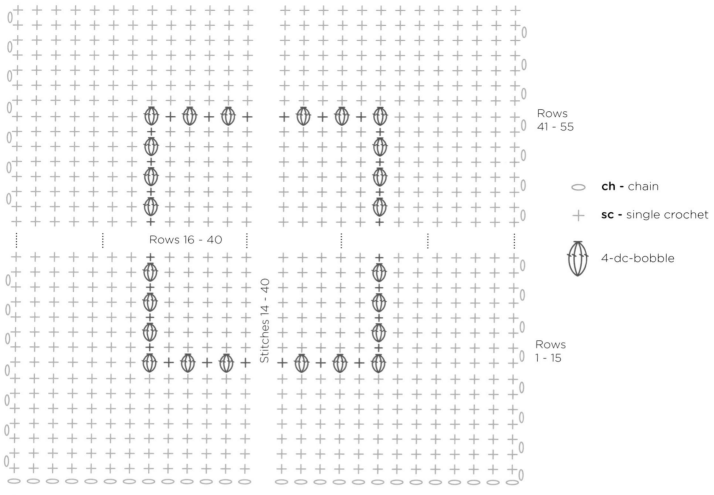

Rows
41 - 55

Rows 16 - 40

Stitches 14 - 40

Rows
1 - 15

○ **ch -** chain

+ **sc -** single crochet

4-dc-bobble

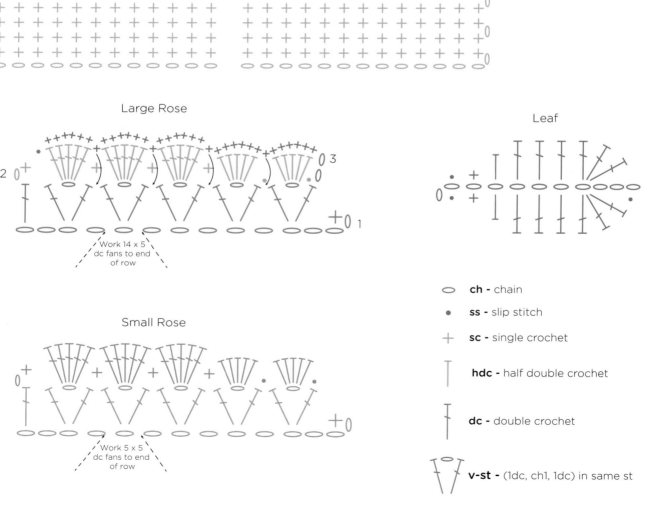

Large Rose

2

3

1

Work 14 x 5
dc fans to end
of row

Small Rose

Work 5 x 5
dc fans to end
of row

Leaf

○ **ch -** chain

• **ss -** slip stitch

+ **sc -** single crochet

hdc - half double crochet

dc - double crochet

v-st - (1dc, ch1, 1dc) in same st

Rose Bag

This simple bag features a beautiful blooming rose. I've used double strands of this fabulous worsted weight cotton yarn held together to give the bag a chunky modern feel, which also means it works up super fast. The rose is worked with two different shades of pink and is added by crocheting into the back loops of the front panel.

MATERIALS

Scheepjes Bloom, 100% cotton, 50g/80m/87yds

Yarn A: Rose 409 x 1 ball

Yarn B: Daisy 423 x 3 balls

Yarn C: Geranium 408 x 1 ball

Blunt ended darning needle

GAUGE

Rnds 1–3 of Front Panel measure approx 4½" (11.5cm) diameter using 6.5mm/K-10.5 crochet hook and two strands of suggested yarn held together.

MEASUREMENTS

Finished Bag Measures: approx. Diameter 8½" (22cm) diameter x 2" (5cm) width/depth (side of bag)

Shoulder Strap: 2" (5cm) wide x 35" (89cm) long.

ABBREVIATIONS

Ch - chain
Sc - single crochet
Blsc - back loop single crochet
Dc - double crochet
Bldc - back loop double crochet
Ss - slip stitch
Rep - repeat
St/s - stitch/es

PATTERN NOTES

- Working with TWO strands of yarn held together, the bag is created from two circular pieces of crochet worked in unturned rounds. The rose on the front panel is created by working stitches into the remaining front loops of rounds 1 and 2. The front and back pieces are then joined by a slip stitch. The strap is then crocheted by re-joining yarn to the side of the bag, then slip stitching back into the other side.

PATTERN STARTS

FRONT PANEL

With yarn A, make a magic ring.

Rnd 1: Ch3 (counts as 1dc here and throughout), 11dc into ring, join with a ss to top of beginning ch 3. Switch to yarn B. Do not turn - 12 sts.

Work into back loops only for rnds 2 and 3 as follows:
Rnd 2: Ch3, 1bldc in same st, 2bldc in each remaining st around, join with a ss to top of beginning ch 3 - 24 bldc.
Rnd 3: Ch3, 2bldc in next st, [1bldc, 2bldc in next st] around, join with a ss to top of beginning ch 3. Switch to yarn C - 36 bldc.

Working through both loops from here on:
Rnd 4: Ch3, 1dc in next st, 2dc in next st, [2dc, 2dc in next st] around, join with a ss to top of beginning ch 3 - 48 dc.
Rnd 5: Ch3, 4dc in same st, skip 3 sts, [5dc in next st, skip 3 sts] around, join with a ss to top of beginning ch 3. Switch to yarn B - 60 dc.
Rnd 6: Ch3, 1dc in each of next 3 sts, 2dc in next st, [4dc, 2dc in next st] around, join with a ss to top of beginning ch 3 - 72 dc.

Working In Rows For Sides Of Bag, Work Into Back Loops Only For Row 1:

Row 1: Ch1 (does NOT count as st here and throughout), 1blsc in same st, 1blsc into each of next 56 sts, Turn.
Row 2: (Working through both loops) Ch1, 1sc into same st, 1sc into each of next 56 sts. Fasten off.

ROSE

Working into remaining front loops of rnds 1 and 2,

using one strand each of yarns A and C held together.

Rnd 1: Join yarns to front loop of any st in rnd 1, ch1 (does not count as st) (1sc, 3dc) into same st, (1sc, 3dc) in each of next 11 sts – do not join but work (1sc 3dc) around post of dc of rnd 2 directly above.
Rnd 2: Working into rnd 2, (1sc, 3dc) in each of next 23 sts, ss to join.
Fasten off and weave in ends.

BACK PANEL

Working through both loops and using two strands of yarn B held together:

Rnd 1: Using Yarn B, make a magic ring, ch3, (counts as 1dc), 11dc into ring, join with a ss to top of beginning ch 3, do not turn - 12 sts.
Rnd 2: Ch3, 1dc in same st, 2dc in each remaining st around, join with a ss to top of beginning ch 3 - 24 dc.
Rnd 3: Ch3, 2dc in next st, [1dc, 2dc in next st] around, join with a ss to top of beginning ch 3 - 36 dc.
Rnd 4: Ch3, 1dc in next st, 2dc in next st, [2dc, 2dc in next st] around, join with a ss to top of beginning ch 3 - 48 dc.
Rnd 5: Ch3, 1dc in each of next 2 sts, 2dc in next st, [3dc, 2dc in next st] around, join with a ss to top of beginning ch 3 - 60 dc.
Rnd 6: Ch3, 1dc in each of next 3 sts, 2dc in next st, [4dc, 2dc in next st] around, join with a ss to top of beginning ch 3 - 72 dc.

Work in rows for sides of bag, working into back loops only for Row 1 as follows:

Row 1: Ch1, 1blsc in same st, 1blsc into each of next 56 sts, turn.
Row 2: (Working through both loops) ch1, 1sc into same st, 1sc into each of next 56 sts.
Fasten off.

JOINING

With right sides together, using two strands of yarn B, join sides of bag using slip stitches into each sc.

STRAP

Row 1: With bag inside out, re-join yarn A, work 5sc across side panel, turn - 5 sc.
Row 2: Ch1 (does not count as st), 1sc in same st, 1sc in each st across, turn - 5sc.

Repeat row 2 until strap measures approx 35" (89cm), re-join to other side by working 5 ss into side panel. check that the strap is not twisted before you join.

Weave in ends, turn bag to right side.

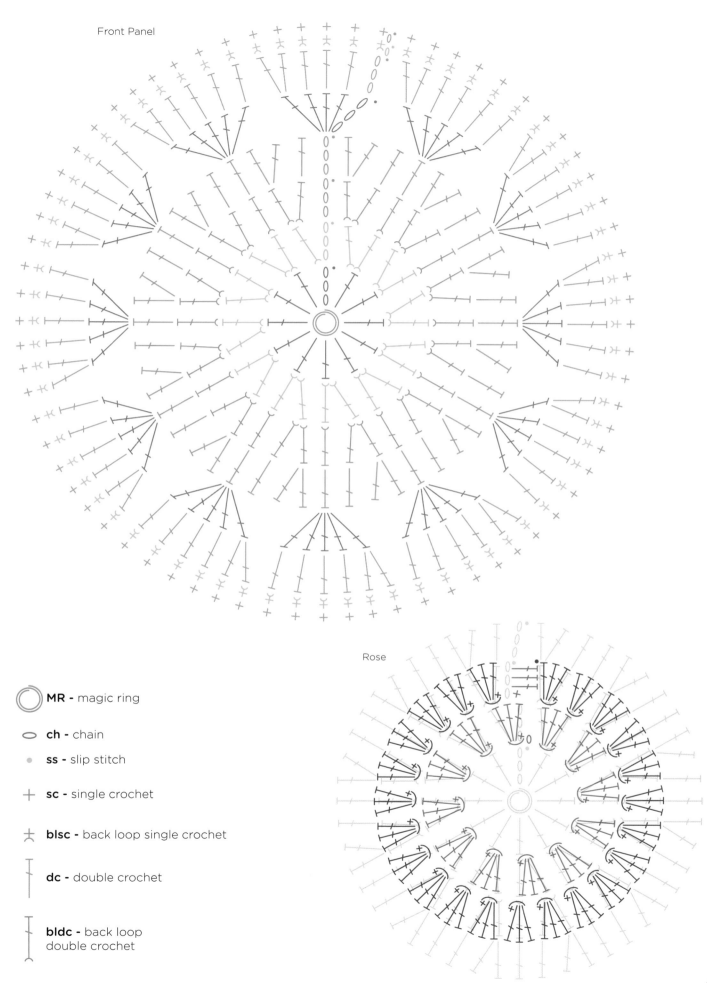

Front Panel

Rose

MR - magic ring

ch - chain

ss - slip stitch

sc - single crochet

blsc - back loop single crochet

dc - double crochet

bldc - back loop double crochet

Back Panel

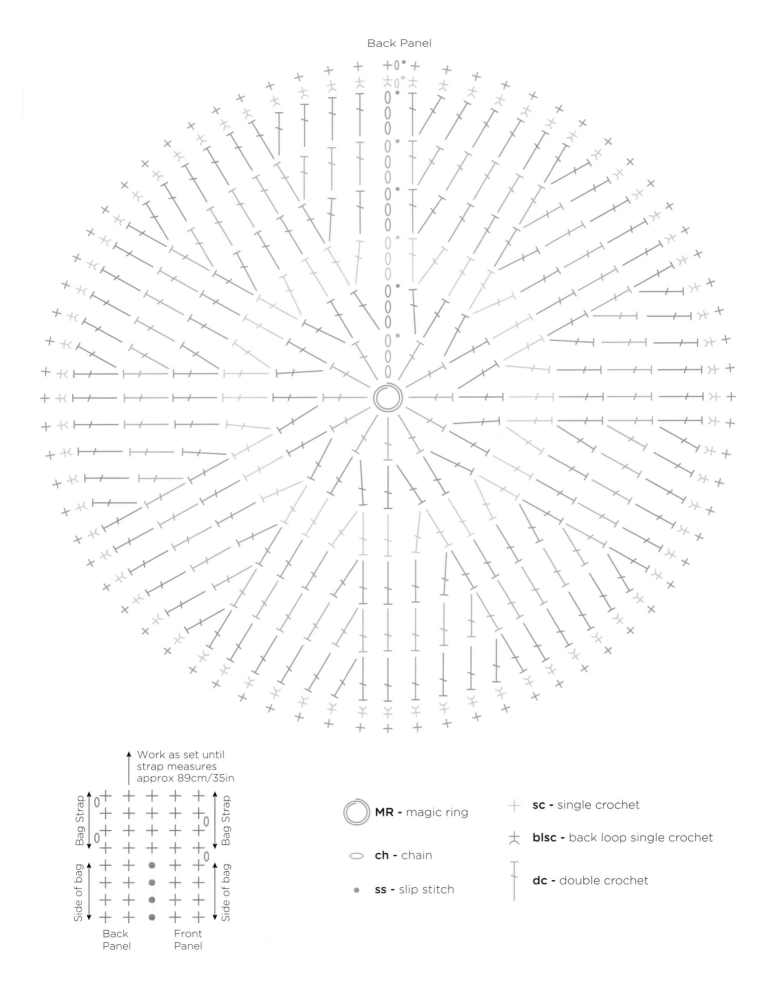

Work as set until
strap measures
approx 89cm/35in

Bag Strap | Side of bag

Back Panel | Front Panel

Bag Strap | Side of bag

MR - magic ring

ch - chain

ss - slip stitch

sc - single crochet

blsc - back loop single crochet

dc - double crochet

Round Rose Cushion

I love watching the roses come to life from mid-spring and miss them when they finally leave the garden in autumn. This rose cushion means I get a bit of that romance all year round.

MATERIALS

Scheepjes Cahlista, 100% cotton, 50g/85m/93yds, shades:

Yarn A: Powder Pink 238 x 1 ball
Yarn B: Sage Green 212 x 1 ball
Yarn C: Old Lace 130 x 3 balls

5mm/US8-H crochet hook

Blunt ended darning needle

41cm/16in round cushion insert

GAUGE

Rnds 1-4 Of Back Panel: Circle with 11.5cm (4½in) diameter worked in pattern using 4.5mm hook and suggested yarn

MEASUREMENTS

Finished Cushion Cover Measures: approx. 15" (38cm) diameter to fit a 16" (41cm) round cushion insert.

ABBREVIATIONS

Ch - chain
Sc – single crochet
Dc – double crochet
Tr – treble crochet
Ss – slip stitch
Rep – repeat
St/s – stitch/es
Sp/s - space/s

SPECIAL STITCHES

Bpsc – Back Post Single Crochet

- Insert hook around the post of the stitch to be worked from back to front (inserting your hook from back to front on the first side of stitch to be worked, then back down from the front to back on the other side of the stitch to be worked) pull up a loop, yarn over, pull through both loops on hook.

Fpsc – Front Post Single Crochet

- Insert hook around the post of the stitch to be worked from front to back (inserting your hook from front to back on the first side of stitch to be worked, then back up from the back to front on the other side of the stitch to be worked) pull up a loop, yarn over, pull through both loops on hook.

Fpcl – Front Post Cluster

- *Yarn over, insert hook around st to be worked from front to back (as for fpsc), yarn over, pull up loop, yarn over, pull through 2 loops; repeat from * twice more (4 loops on hook), yarn over, pull through remaining 4 loops on hook.

5dc-cl – 5 Double Crochet Cluster

- *Yarn over, insert hook into st or sp to be worked, yarn over, pull up a loop, yarn over, pull through 2 loops on hook; repeat from * four more times (until 6 loops on hook), yarn over, pull through all loops on hook.

V-st

- (1dc, ch1, 1dc) in same st.

PATTERN NOTES

- Cushion Cover is made in two parts (front panel and back panel), which are then joined.

PATTERN STARTS

FRONT PANEL

Rnd 1: Using yarn A, 8sc into magic ring, join with ss to first sc - 8sc.
Rnd 2: Ch5 (counts as 1dc, ch2), (1dc, ch2) in each st around, join with ss to 3rd of beginning ch 5 - 8dc, 8 x ch2-sps.
Rnd 3: Ch1 (does not count as a stitch here and throughout), 1sc in same st, *(1dc, 3tr, 1dc) in ch2-sp, 1sc in next st; rep from * six more times, (1dc, 3tr, 1dc) in last ch2-sp, join with ss to first sc - 48 sts.
Rnd 4: Ch1, 1bpsc around sc (directly below) from rnd 3, (working behind the petals from rnd 3) *ch3, 1bpsc around next sc; rep from * 6 more times, ch3, ss into first bpsc - 8 bpsc, 8 x ch3-sps.
Rnd 5: Ch1, 1fpsc around first bpsc, *(2dc, 3tr, 2dc) in ch3-sp, 1fpsc around next bpsc; rep from * six more times, (2dc, 3tr, 2dc) in last ch3-sp, ss into first fpsc. Fasten off yarn A - 64 sts.
Rnd 6: Join yarn B into middle tr of any rnd 5 petal, 1sc in same st, *ch3, skip 3 sts, 1fpcl around fpsc, ch3, skip 3 sts, 1sc in next st (middle tr of petal); rep from * six more times, ch3, skip 3 sts, 1fpcl around fpsc, ch3, join with a ss to beginning sc - 8 fpcl, 8sc.
Rnd 7: Ch4 (counts as 1dc, 1ch), 1dc in same st, *ch3, 5dc-cl (working 2dc in ch3-sp, 1dc in fpcl, 2dc in next ch3-sp), ch3, V-st in next sc; rep from * six more times, ch3, 5dc-cl (working 2dc in ch3-sp, 1dc in fpcl, 2dc in next ch3-sp), ch3, ss into 3rd of beginning ch 4. Fasten off yarn B - 8 x 5dc-cl, 8 V-sts, 16 x ch3-sps.
Rnd 8: Attach yarn C to any 5dc-cl from rnd 7, ch3 (counts as 1dc), *4dc in ch3-sp, 1dc in next st, 2dc in ch1-sp, 1dc in next st, 4dc in ch3-sp, 1dc in 5dc-cl; rep from * 6 more times, 4dc in ch3-sp, 1dc in next st, 2dc in ch1-sp, 1dc in next st, 4dc in ch3-sp, join with ss to top of beginning ch 3. Fasten off yarn C - 104 sts.
Rnd 9: Attach yarn A to any st, 1sc in each st around, join with ss to beginning sc. Fasten off yarn A.
Rnd 10: Attach yarn C to any st, ch3 (counts as 1dc here and throughout), 1dc in each st around, join with ss to beginning ch 3.
Rnd 11: Ch3, 6dc, 2dc in next st, [7dc, 2dc in next st] around, join with ss to beginning ch 3. Fasten off yarn C - 117 sts.
Rnd 12: Rep rnd 9.
Rnd 13: Attach yarn C to any st, ch3, 7dc, 2dc in next st, [8dc, 2dc in next st] around, join with ss to beginning ch 3 - 130 sts.
Rnd 14: Ch3, 8dc, 2dc in next st, [9dc, 2dc in next st] around, join with ss to beginning ch 3 - 143 sts.
Rnd 15: Ch3, 9dc, 2dc in next st, [10dc, 2dc in next st] around, join with ss to beginning ch 3 - 156 sts.
Fasten off and weave in ends.

BACK PANEL

Rnd 1: Using yarn A, 12dc in magic ring, join with ss to beginning dc - 12dc.

Rnd 2: Ch3 (counts as 1dc here and throughout) 1dc in same st, 2dc in each st around, join with ss in beginning ch 3 - 24 sts.

Rnd 3: Ch3, 2dc in next st, [1dc, 2dc in next st] around, join with ss in beginning ch 3 - 36 sts.

Rnd 4: Ch3, 1dc, 2dc in next st, [2dc, 2dc in next st] around, join with ss in beginning ch 3 - 48 sts.

Rnd 5: Ch3, 2dc, 2dc in next st, [3dc, 2dc in next st] around, join with ss in beginning ch 3 - 60 sts.

Rnd 6: Ch3, 3dc, 2dc in next st, [4dc, 2dc in next st] around, join with ss in beginning ch 3 - 72 sts.

Rnd 7: Ch3, 4dc, 2dc in next st, [5dc, 2dc in next st] around, join with ss in beginning ch 3 - 84 sts.

Rnd 8: Ch3, 5dc, 2dc in next st, [6dc, 2dc in next st] around, join with ss in beginning ch 3 - 96 sts.

Rnd 9: Ch3, 6dc, 2dc in next st, [7dc, 2dc in next st] around, join with ss in beginning ch 3 - 108 sts.

Rnd 10: Ch3, 7dc, 2dc in next st, [8dc, 2dc in next st] around, join with ss in beginning ch 3 - 120 sts.

Rnd 11: Ch3, 8dc, 2dc in next st, [9dc, 2dc in next st] around, join with ss in beginning ch 3 - 132 sts.

Rnd 12: Ch3, 9dc, 2dc in next st, [10dc, 2dc in next st] around, join with ss in beginning ch 3 - 144 sts.

Rnd 13: Ch3, 10dc, 2dc in next st, [11dc, 2dc in next st] around, join with ss in beginning ch 3 - 156 sts.

TO JOIN

Place both panels with wrong sides together and right sides facing up, using yarn C, join panels by working 1sc in each st around (working through both panels). Insert cushion filler when you are half way around and then continue to join both panels, join with ss to first sc.

Edging Rnd: Switch to yarn A, ch1, 1sc, skip 1 st, 3dc in next st, 1dc in next st, 3dc in next st, skip 1 st, *1sc in next st, skip 1 st, 3dc in next st, 1dc in next st, 3dc in next st, skip 1 st; rep from * around, join with ss to beg sc.

TO FINISH

Fasten off and weave in ends.

Note: if you'd like to make a cushion cover for a bigger insert, continue working rounds of dc on both panels, increasing by 12 sts each row.

Front Panel

Edging

Legend

MR - magic ring

ch - chain

ss - slip stitch

sc - single crochet

FPsc - front post single crochet

BPsc - back post single crochet

dc - double crochet

tr - treble crochet

5dc-cl - 5 double crochet cluster

FPcl - front post 3 double crochet bobble

V-st - (1dc, ch1, 1dc) in same st

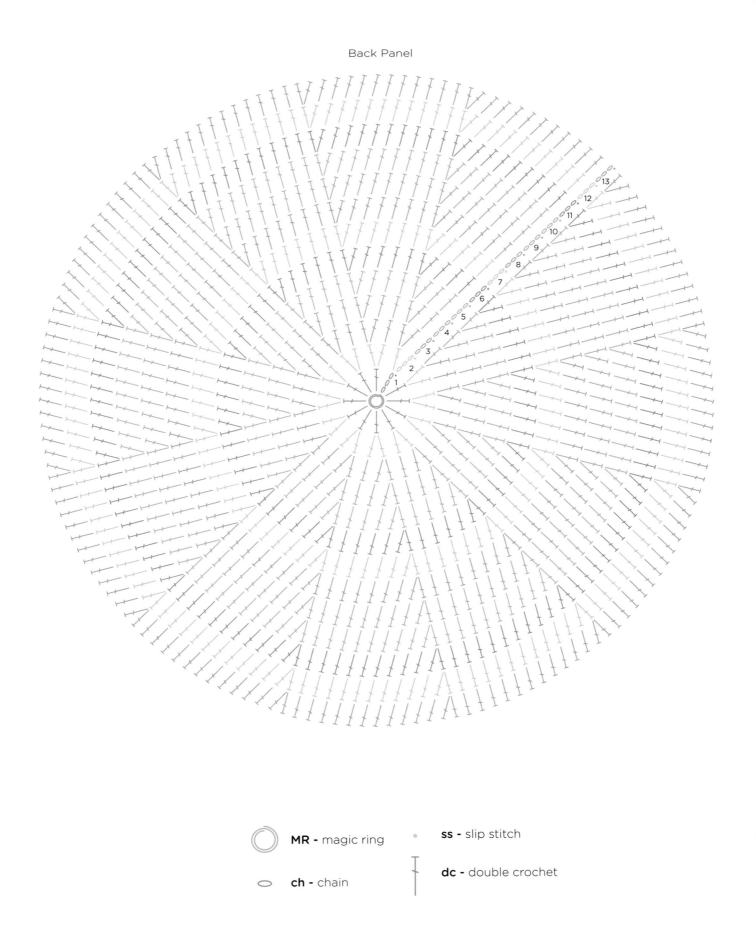

MR - magic ring

ch - chain

ss - slip stitch

dc - double crochet

Ruffle Shawlette

I love crocheting ruffles. I could add them to anything. In this shawlette pattern, they are the star of the show; turning a very simple design into something elegant. Made using Merino yarn this shawlette is perfect for warming your shoulders or snuggling into as a scarf.

MATERIALS

Scheepjes Our Tribe, 70% Merino superwash, 30% polyamide, 100g/420m/459yds

Yarn A: Motivate 983 x 2 balls
Yarn B: Miss Neriss 966 x 1 ball

3.5mm/US4E crochet hook

Blunt ended darning needle

GAUGE

20 sts x 10 rows worked in double crochet to measure 4 x4" (10 x 10cm) square using suggested yarn and 3.5mm/US4E hook.

MEASUREMENTS

Finished Shawlette Measures: approx. 63" (160cm) in length (point to point) x depth (at center) 13" (33cm)

ABBREVIATIONS

Ch – chain
Sc – single crochet
Dc – double crochet
Ss – slip stitch
Rep – repeat
St/s – stitch/es

SPECIAL STITCHES

Dc2tog

- Yarn over, insert hook into st, yarn over, pull up a loop (3 loops on hook), yarn over, pull through 2 loops (2 loops remaining on hook), yarn over, insert hook into next st, yarn over, pull up a loop, (4 loops remaining on hook) yarn over, pull through 2 loops (3 loops remaining on hook), yarn over, pull through all remaining loops on hook.

Dc2tog at Beginning of Row

- Ch2 (counts as first half of dc), yarn over, insert hook into next st, yarn over, pull up a loop (3 loops remaining on hook), yarn over, pull through 2 loops on hook (2 loops remaining on hook), yarn over, pull through remaining loops on hook.

PATTERN NOTES

- Shawlette is worked in rows, from point to point, using increases and decreases to create shape. All the increases and decreases should be worked along the same edge of shawl. Ruffle border is then added afterwards. Shawl does not require blocking.

PATTERN STARTS

Row 1: Using yarn A, ch5 (counts as 2ch, 1dc), 1dc into fourth ch from hook, 1dc into last ch, turn - 3 sts.
Row 2: Ch3 (counts as 1dc here and throughout) 1dc in next st, 2dc in last st. - 4 sts.
Row 3: Ch3, 1dc in same st (increase made), 1dc in each st along, turn - 5 sts.
Row 4: Ch3, 1dc in each st until last st, 2dc in last st (increase made), turn - 6 sts.
Rows 5-63: Rep rows 3 and 4 until there are 65 sts.
Rows 64-94: Ch3, 1dc in each st along, turn.
Row 95: Dc2tog (see Special Stitches for decrease at beginning of row), 1dc in each st to end, turn - 64 sts.
Row 96: Ch3, 1dc in each st to last 2 sts, dc2tog, turn - 63 sts.
Rows 97-157: Rep rows 95 and 96 until 2 sts remain.
Fasten off yarn A.

EDGING

Row 1: Re-attach yarn A to last dc of row 157, ch1 (does not count as a st), 1sc in same st, skip next dc, (you will now be working along curved edge of shawl, working around posts of dc's), 2sc into edge of each row along to following point of shawl, skip 1 remaining ch loop of foundation ch, 1sc in beginning ch loop of foundation ch. Turn. Fasten off yarn A - 284 sts.

Row 2: Attach yarn A to last sc of previous row, ch1 (does not count as a st), 1sc in same st, 1sc in each of next 2 sts, 3dc in each st along to last 3 sts, 1sc in each of last 3 sts, turn.
Row 3: Ch1 (does not count as a st), 1sc in each of next 3 sts, 1dc in each st to last 3 sts, 1sc in each of last 3 sts, turn.
Row 4: Rep edging row 3.
Fasten off, weave in ends.

⬭ **ch** - chain

✛ **sc** - single crochet

✝ **dc** - double crochet

⋀ **dc2tog** - double crochet decrease

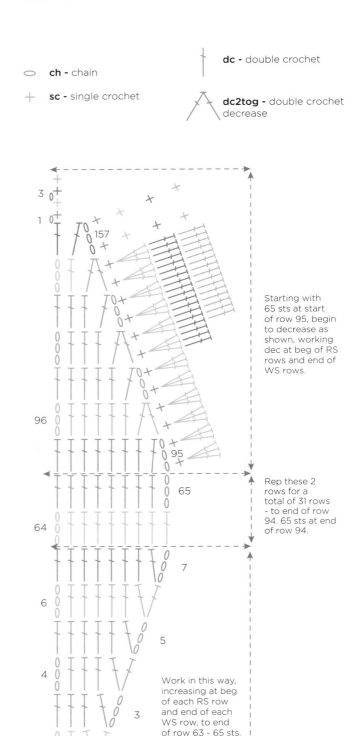

Starting with 65 sts at start of row 95, begin to decrease as shown, working dec at beg of RS rows and end of WS rows.

Rep these 2 rows for a total of 31 rows - to end of row 94. 65 sts at end of row 94.

Work in this way, increasing at beg of each RS row and end of each WS row, to end of row 63 - 65 sts.

Teapot Cosy

Mostly I drink my tea from a mug with one foot out of the door but when I do find the time to slow down a pot of tea is the perfect remedy for a busy day. This teapot cosy evokes the promise of a slowly brewed cup of tea and with it time to daydream, catch up with friends and family or or even a good book. I've taken color inspiration from my favourite vintage tea set, but experiment to your heart's desire. I can't promise you ten minutes of peace but I can promise you that your teapot will look beautiful!

MATERIALS

Scheepjes Merino Soft, 50% superwash Merino wool, 25% microfibre, 25% acrylic, 50g/105m/114yds

Yarn A: Raphael 602 x 1 ball
Yarn B: Titian 647 x 1 ball
Yarn C: Bennett 633 x 1 ball
Yarn D: Caravaggio 642 x 1 ball

4mm/G-6 crochet hook

Blunt ended darning needle

GAUGE

18 sts and 8 rows over main pattern to measure 4 x 4" (10 x 10cm) using 4mm/G-6 hook or size required to obtain gauge.

MEASUREMENTS

Finished Tea Pot Cosy Measures: approx. 7¼" (18.5cm) width x 8" (20cm) height.

To fit a standard teapot 6" (15cm) diameter x 6" (15cm) tall.

ABBREVIATIONS

Ch - chain
Sc - single crochet
Dc - double crochet
Fldc - front loop double crochet
Bldc - back loop double crochet
RS/WS - right side/wrong side
Rep - repeat
Sp/s - space/s

PATTERN NOTES

- Teapot cosy is worked in two pieces. The ruffles are then added to each piece in rows. Both pieces are then joined, leaving gaps for the spout and handle.
- Ch3 at start of row counts as 1dc.
- Ch1 at start of row does NOT count as st.

PATTERN STARTS

TEA COSY SIDE (MAKE 2)

With yarn A, ch35.

Row 1 (RS): 1dc in 4th ch from hook, 1dc into each ch along, turn - 33dc
Row 2 (WS): (Work in front loops only), Ch3 (counts as 1dc here and throughout), 1fldc in each st along, turn - 33fldc.
Row 3: (Work in back loops only), Ch3, 1bldc in each st along, turn - 33bldc.
Rows 4-13: Rep rows 2 and 3 five more times. Fasten off. With RS of work facing, join yarn B to first dc of row 13. Working through both loops of each st continue as follows:
Row 14 (RS): Ch3, *skip next st, (1dc, ch1, 1dc) in next st, skip 1 st, 1dc in next st; rep from * to end of row, turn - 9dc, 8 groups of (1dc, 1ch, 1dc).
Row 15 (WS): Ch3, *skip next st, (2dc, ch2, 2dc) in ch1-sp, skip next st, 1dc in next st; rep from * to end of row, turn.
Row 16: Ch1 (does not count as st), 1sc in same st, *skip 2 sts, 7dc in ch2-sp, skip next 2 sts, 1sc in next st; rep from * to end of row. Fasten off yarn B.

RUFFLES

Continue working into remaining loops from fl/bl double crochet of rows 12 down to (and including) row 3 as follows:
With RS facing, join yarn C to first dc of row 12 (working in remaining loops):
Row 1: Rep row 14.
Row 2: Ch1 (does not count as st), *skip 1 st, 5dc in ch1-sp, skip 1 st, 1sc in next st; rep from * to end of row. Fasten off yarn.
Rep rows 1 and 2 on every row of tea cosy leaving 2 rows at bottom of cosy unworked. Switching colors

every two rows as follows:
Rows 12 and 11: Yarn C.
Rows 10 and 9: Yarn D.
Rows 8 and 7: Yarn B.
Rows 6 and 5: Yarn C.
Rows 4 and 3: Yarn D.
Fasten off, weave in ends.

Repeat for second side of tea cosy. Weave in ends.

FINISHING

TO JOIN

With WS facing, sew both pieces of cosy together using yarn A and a darning needle. Be careful not to work through any ruffles. Sew cosy together ½" (1.5cm) from bottom, leaving 3¼" (8cm) unsewn for handle and spout, then joining to top of cosy, switch to yarn B to join rows 14-16.

TIE

Using one strand of each of yarns B, C and D held together, 100ch.
Fasten off and thread yarns through blunt ended needle. Weave tie in and out of every second double crochet in row 13 of tea cosy.
Weave in ends.

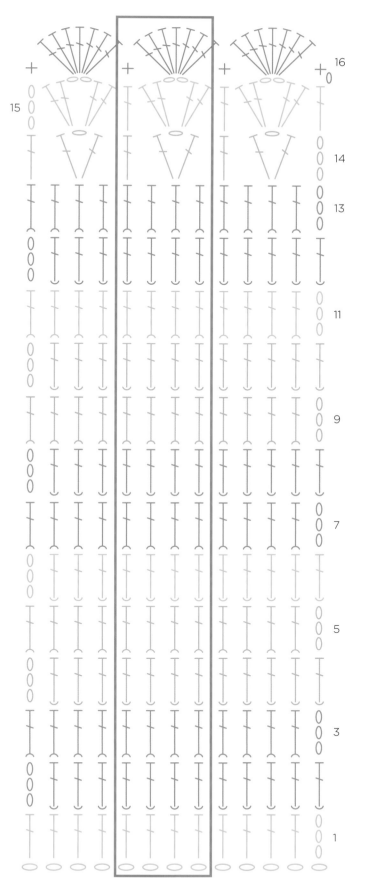

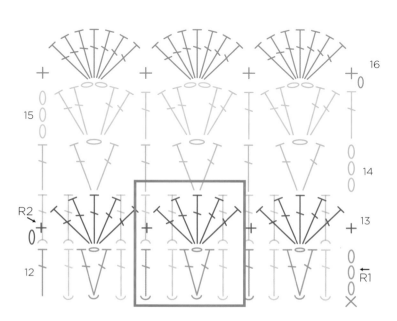

ch - chain

sc - single crochet

dc - double crochet

bldc - back loop double crochet

fldc - front loop double crochet

pattern repeat

R1: Ruffle Row 1
(shown in green)

R2: Ruffle Row 2
(shown in blue)

Chart shows first two rows only of ruffle pattern with side pattern underneath. Start with RS facing and join yarn at right hand edge of side row 12 (indicated by red cross). Repeat two row ruffle pattern down the side piece from rows 12 to 3 as indicated in instructions. Do not work ruffles on side rows 1 and 2.

Read odd (RS) rows from R to L and even (WS) rows from L to R up to end of row 13.

Posy Top

This top is made up of two rectangular panels that are worked sideways then seamed together to create a beautiful v-neck top. The simple construction makes it a good project if you are new to garment making. Perfect for summer days when you want to keep the sun off your shoulders.

MATERIALS

Scheepjes Soft Fun 60% cotton, 40% acrylic, 50g/140m/153yds

Yarn A: 2621 x 1 ball

Yarn B: 2618 x 1 ball

Yarn C: 2426 x 5 (6, 7) balls

4.5mm/US7 crochet hook

Blunt ended darning needle

GAUGE

Work 13.5 sts and 8 rows in pattern (equivalent to 4.5 granny clusters) to measure 4" x 4" (10 x 10cm) using 4.5mm/US7 hook or size required to obtain gauge.

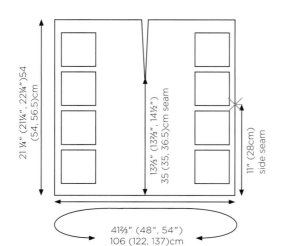

21¼" (21¼", 22¼")54 (54, 56.5)cm

13⅞" (13⅞", 14½") 35 (35, 36.5)cm seam

11" (28cm) side seam

41⅔" (48", 54") 106 (122, 137)cm

MEASUREMENTS

To Fit	Finished Chest Approx		Length Approx	
	cm	inch	cm	inch
XS/S	106	41⅔	54	21¼
M/L	122	48	54	21¼
XL/2XL	137	54	56.5	22¼

ABBREVIATIONS

Ch - chain
Sc - single crochet
Hdc - half double crochet
Dc - double crochet
Cl - cluster
Tr-cl - treble crochet cluster
Ss - slip stitch
Rep - repeat
St/s - stitches
Sp - space/s

PATTERN NOTES

- Top is made from two rectangle panels of crochet which, when finished, are joined to make a center seam, then joined along the sides to create arm holes. The top is designed to be loose fitting (boxy) with between 6-10" (15-25cm) of positive ease.

- Change color by working last pull through of previous stitch in new yarn color ready for next stitch.

SPECIAL STITCHES

2tr-cl - 2 treble crochet cluster

- *Yarn over twice, insert hook in st, yarn over and pull up a loop (4 loops on hook), [yarn over, pull through 2 loops] twice (2 loops on hook): rep from * once more; yarn over and pull through all 3 loops on hook.

3tr-cl - 3 treble crochet cluster

- *Yarn over twice, insert hook in st, yarn over and pull pull up a loop (4 loops on hook), [yarn over, draw through 2 loops] twice (2 loops on hook): rep from * twice more; yarn over and draw through all 4 loops on hook.

PATTERN STARTS

PANELS (MAKE TWO)

FIRST MOTIF

With Yarn A, ch4, join with ss to form a ring.

Rnd 1: Ch1 (does not count as st), 8sc into ring, join with ss, switch to yarn B - 8 sts.
Rnd 2: Ch3 (counts as first st of beginning tr-cl) 2tr-cl in same st, ch3, [3tr-cl in next sc, ch3] seven times, join with ss to top of first cl, fasten off yarn A - 8 x 3tr-clusters.
Rnd 3: Join yarn C to any ch3-sp, ch3 (counts as 1dc), (2dc, ch3, 3dc) in same ch3-sp, ch1, 3hdc in next ch3-sp, ch1, * (3dc, ch3, 3dc) in next ch3-sp, ch1, 3hdc in next sp, ch1; rep from * twice more, join with ss to top of beginning ch 3 - 36 sts, 4 x ch3-sps, 8 x ch1-sps.

Rnd 4: Ch4 (counts as 1dc, ch1) *(3dc, ch3, 3dc) in corner ch3-sp, ch1, [3dc in next ch-sp, ch1] twice; rep from * twice more, (3dc, ch3, 3dc) in corner sp, ch1, 3dc in next ch-sp, ch1, 2dc in next ch1-sp, ss to third of beginning ch 4 - 48 sts, 4 x ch3-sps, 12 x ch2-sps.

MOTIFS 2-8

Rep Rnds 1-3 of First Motif.
Now join each square motif along one side as you work the fourth row – to make a row of 8 joined motifs:

Rnd 4: Ch4 (counts as 1dc, ch1) *(3dc, ch3, 3dc) in corner sp, ch1, [3dc in next ch1-sp, ch1] twice; rep from * once more, (3dc, ch1,) in corner sp, join with ss into corner ch3-sp of motif to be joined (ch1, 3dc) back into same corner sp, *ss into next ch1-sp of motif to be joined, 3dc into ch1-sp of working motif; rep from * once more, ss into next ch1-sp of motif to be joined, (3dc, ch1) into corner sp of working motif, join with ss to corner sp of motif to be joined, (ch1, 3dc) back into corner ch3-sp of working motif, ch1, 3dc into next ch1-sp, ch1, 2dc into last ch-sp, ss to 3rd of beginning ch 4.

FRONT EDGE ROWS

Now work in rows along top of joined motifs as follows:

Row 1: With RS of long strip of joined motifs facing, rejoin yarn A in top right hand corner ch3-sp, ch3 (counts as 1dc) 1dc in same ch3-sp, work 1dc in each st and ch1-sp to next corner, 2dc in corner, *1dc in corner of NEXT motif, work 1dc in each st and ch1-sp to next corner, 2dc in corner; rep from * in each motif to end of strip, turn - 145 dc. Switch to Yarn C.
Row 2: Ch3 (counts as 1dc here and throughout), skip two sts, [3dc in next st, skip 2 sts] to last st, 1dc in last st, turn - 143dc.
Row 3: Ch3, 1dc in sp before next 3 dc group, [3dc in next sp between 3 dc groups] to last sp, 1dc in sp between 3 dc group and dc, 1dc top of ch 3, turn - 142dc.
Row 4: Ch3, [3dc in next sp between 3 dc groups] to last sp, 1dc in last st, turn - 143dc.
Rep last two rows 4 (4, 5) more times (total of 10 (12, 14) rows). Fasten off.

SIDE EDGE ROWS

Turn piece and work along second long side of rows of motifs as follows:

Sizes S and M Only

Work rows 1 to 3 (4) as for Front Edge Rows.

Size L Only

Work rows 1 to 4 then work row 1 again as for Front Edge Rows. Fasten off.

JOINING

Place panels side by side lengthways (with flower motifs on outsides) see diagram. Join using yarn C with whip stitch along center seam for 13⅔" (13⅔", 14½"), (35 (35, 36.5)cm), leave 15" (15", 15½"), (38 (38, 40)cm) for neck opening, then stitch remaining 13⅔" (13⅔", 14½"), (35 (35, 36.5)cm).

Fold piece in half width ways, sew sides together 11" (28cm) from bottom on both sides to create arm holes – see diagram.

EDGING

Using Yarn C work 1 (1, 6) rows of sc evenly along bottom of garment.

42½" (42½", 44½")
108 (108, 113)cm

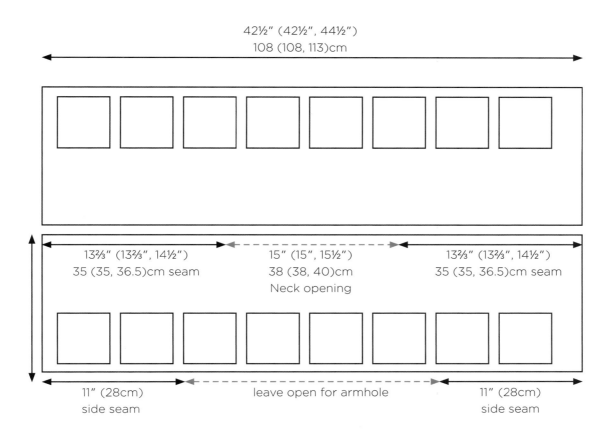

13⅔" (13⅔", 14½")
35 (35, 36.5)cm seam

15" (15", 15½")
38 (38, 40)cm
Neck opening

13⅔" (13⅔", 14½")
35 (35, 36.5)cm seam

11" (28cm)
side seam

leave open for armhole

11" (28cm)
side seam

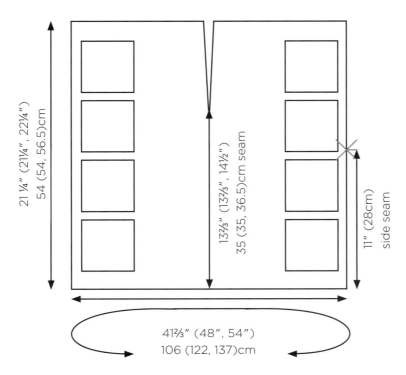

21¼" (21¼", 22¼")
54 (54, 56.5)cm

13⅔" (13⅔", 14½")
35 (35, 36.5)cm seam

11" (28cm)
side seam

41⅔" (48", 54")
106 (122, 137)cm

Body Side Rep these two rows for pattern

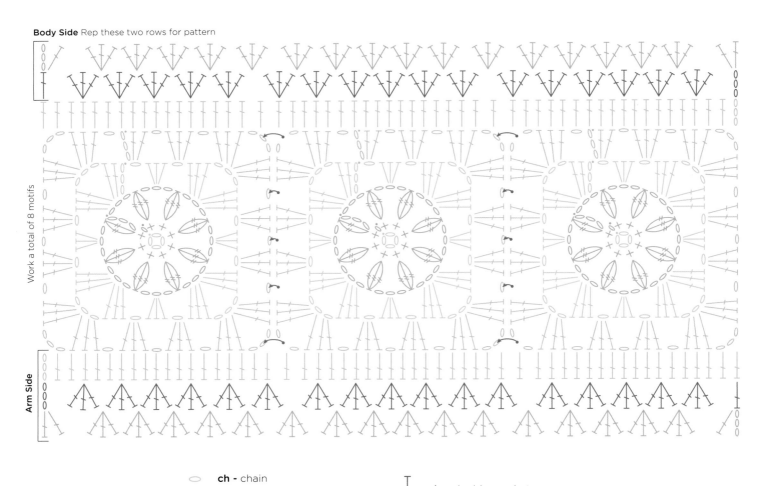

Work a total of 8 motifs

Arm Side

ch - chain

ss - slip stitch

joining ss worked into first motif

sc - single crochet

hdc - half double crochet

dc - double crochet

3tr-cl - 3 treble crochet cluster

2tr-cl - 2 treble crochet cluster

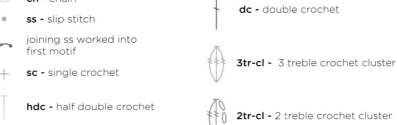

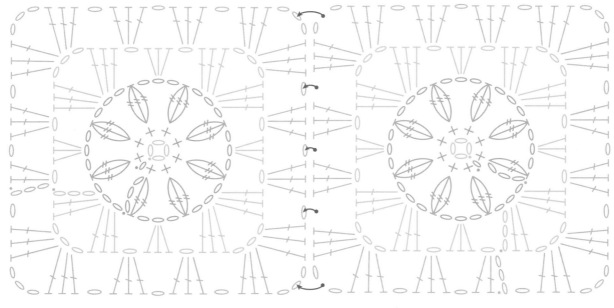

Second and subsequent Motifs

Vintage Motif Cushion

Inspired by delicate vintage motifs, this pretty cushion has been given a modern twist by working the granny stitch border in pinks and mustard, one of my favorite color combinations.

MATERIALS

Scheepjes Catona, 100% cotton, 50g/125m/137yds,

Yarn A: Old Lace 130 x 3 balls
Yarn B: Old Rose 408 x 1 ball
Yarn C: Peach 523 x 1 ball
Yarn D: Topaz 179 x 1 ball

3.5mm/US4E crochet hook

Blunt ended darning needle

16 x 16" (41 x 41cm) square cushion filler

GAUGE

Rnds 1 – 5 of back panel measure a square 4¼ x 4¼" (11 x 11cm) using suggested yarn and 3.5mm/US4E hook.

MEASUREMENTS

Finished Cushion Cover Measures:
approx. 15½" x 15½" x (39 x 39cm), to fit a 16" (40cm) cushion pad

ABBREVIATIONS

Ch - chain
Sc – single crochet
Dc – double crochet
Ss – slip stitch
Rep – repeat
St/s – stitch/es
Sp/s - space/s

SPECIAL STITCHES

Beg 3dc-cl

- Ch2 (counts as first half of first dc), *yarn over, insert hook into same st, yarn over, pull up a loop, yarn over, pull through 2 loops, (2 loops on hook); repeat from once more (3 loops on hook), yarn over, pull through all 3 remaining loops.

3dc-cl

- *Yarn over, insert hook into st, yarn over, pull up a loop, yarn over, pull through 2 loops on hook (2 loops on hook); repeat from * twice more, (4 loops on hook), yarn over, pull through all 4 remaining loops.

PATTERN NOTES

- Four motifs are made separately then joined horizontally and vertically to create a 2 x 2 motif square using either a crochet ss or sewn. Stitches are then worked around joined motifs. The back panel is a simple granny square. Front and back panels are joined with single crochet stitches.

PATTERN STARTS

FRONT PANEL

MOTIFS (MAKE 4)

With yarn A, make magic ring.
Rnd 1: 12dc in ring, join with ss - 12 sts.
Rnd 2: *Beg 3dc-cl into first st, ch1, 3dc-cl into next st, ch1, 3dc-cl into next st, ch5; rep from * three more times (work 3dc-cl instead of Beg 3dc-cl at beg of each rep), ss to top of first 3dc-cl - 12 x 3dc-cl sts, 4 x ch5.
Rnd 3: Ss in next ch1-sp, *Beg 3dc-cl in same sp, ch1, 3dc-cl in next ch1-sp, ch2, (2dc, ch3, 2dc) in ch5-sp, ch2; rep from * three more times (work 3dc-cl instead of Beg 3dc-cl at beg of each rep), ss to top of first 3dc-cl. (8 x 3dc-cl, 16dc)
Rnd 4: Ss in next ch1-sp, *Beg 3dc-cl in same sp, ch2, 1dc in next ch2-sp, ch2, (3dc, ch3, 3dc) in ch3-sp, ch2, 1dc in next ch2-sp, ch2; rep from * three more times, (work 3dc-cl instead of Beg 3dc-cl at beg of each rep), ss to top of first 3dc-cl, fasten off and weave in ends - 4 x 3dc-cl, 32dc.

Join all four motifs using yarn A, either by sewing or slip stitching into each st, so motifs are joined horizontally and vertically to create a 2 x 2 motif square. With right sides facing, work joining stitches through both corresponding stitches, working through back loops only.

Re-join yarn A to any corner ch3-sp of joined motifs.

Rnd 1: *Ch3 (counts as 1dc), (1dc, ch3, 2dc) in same sp, 1dc in each of next 3 sts, 2dc in ch2-sp, skip 1 st, 2dc in next ch2-sp, skip next cl st, 2dc in ch2-sp, skip next st, 2dc in next ch2-sp, 1dc in each of next 3 sts, 1dc in each of next 3 sts (next joined motif), 2dc in ch2-sp, skip next st, 2dc in next ch2-sp, skip cl st, 2dc in ch2-sp, skip next st, 2dc in next ch2-sp, 1dc in each of next 3 sts; rep from * three more times (work 1dc instead of ch3 at beg of each rep), join with a ss to beginning ch 3. Fasten off yarn A - 128 sts.
Rnd 2: Using yarn B, join to any corner ch3-sp, **ch3 (counts as 1dc), (2dc, ch3, 3dc) in same sp, *skip next 2 sts, 3dc in next st; repeat from * until corner ch3-sp, rep from ** three more times (work 1dc instead of ch3 at beg of each rep), join with a ss to beginning ch 3, turn - 48 groups of 3dc.
Rnd 3: **Ch3 (counts as 1dc), 2dc in sp before next group of dc's, *skip 3 dc, 3dc in sp before next group of dc's; rep from * until corner ch3-sp, (3dc, ch3, 3dc) in corner sp; rep from ** three more times, (work 1dc instead of ch3 at beg of each rep), ss to beginning ch 3. Fasten off yarn B - 52 groups of 3dc.
Rnd 4: Using yarn C, rep rnd 2 - 56 groups of 3dc.
Rnd 5: Rep rnd 3 - 60 groups of 3dc.
Rnd 6: Using yarn D, rep rnd 2 - 64 groups of 3dc.
Rnd 7: Rep rnd 3 - 68 groups of 3dc.
Rnd 8: Using yarn B, rep rnd 2 - 72 groups of 3dc.

Fasten off and weave in ends.

BACK PANEL

With yarn A, make magic ring.
Rnd 1: Ch3 (counts as 1dc here and throughout), 2dc in ring, ch3, (3dc, ch3) three times in ring, join with ss to beginning ch 3, turn - 4 groups of 3dc = 12 sts.
Rnd 2: Ch3, (2dc, ch3, 3dc) into corner ch3-sp, *skip 3 dc, (3dc, ch3, 3dc) into next corner ch3-sp; rep from * twice more, join with ss to beginning ch 3, turn - 8 groups of 3dc = 24 sts.
Rnd 3: Ch3, 2dc in same space, *(3dc, ch3, 3dc) in corner ch3-sp, 3dc in space between next two 3 dc groups; rep from * twice more, (3dc, ch3, 3dc) in corner ch3-sp, join with ss to beginning ch 3, turn - 12 groups of 3dc = 36 sts.
Rnd 4: Ch3, 2dc in same space, *(3dc, ch3, 3dc) in corner ch3-sp, 3dc in each sp between 3 dc groups to next corner ch3-sp; rep from * twice more, (3dc, ch3, 3dc) in corner ch3-sp, 3dc in sp between each 3 dc group to end of rnd,

ss to beginning ch 3, turn - 16 groups of 3 dc = 48 sts.

Rnds 5–18: Work in pattern as set by rnd 4 working (3dc, ch3, 3dc) in each corner ch3-sp, and 3dc in sp between each 3 dc group.

Back Panel Stitch Count

Rnd 5 – 20 groups of 3dc = 60 sts.
Rnd 6 – 24 groups pf 3dc = 72 sts.
Rnd 7 – 28 groups of 3dc = 84 sts.
Rnd 8 – 32 groups of 3dc = 96 sts.
Rnd 9 – 36 groups of 3dc = 108 sts.
Rnd 10 – 40 groups of 3dc = 120 sts.
Rnd 11 – 44 groups of 3dc = 13 sts.
Rnd 12 – 48 groups of 3dc = 144 sts.
Rnd 13 – 52 groups of 3dc = 156 sts.

Rnd 14 – 56 groups of 3dc = 168 sts.
Rnd 15 – 60 groups of 3dc = 180 sts.
Rnd 16 – 64 groups of 3dc = 192 sts.
Rnd 17 – 68 groups of 3dc = 204 sts.
Rnd 18 – 72 groups of 3dc = 216 sts.

JOINING

Using yarn B, with right side of front panel facing out, place both panels together and join by working 1sc into each st (working through corresponding stitches on both panels), work 3sc into each corner space. Insert cushion pad after three sides are joined. Join with a ss to beginning sc.

| **MR -** magic ring | • **ss -** slip stitch | ⊤ **dc -** double crochet | **3dc-cl -** 3 double crochet cluster |
| **ch -** chain | + **sc -** single crochet | | **beg 3dc-cl -** beginning 3 double crochet cluster |

Front Panel Motif

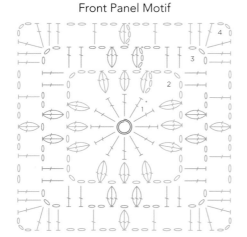

Back

Work rounds in this way, working 3dc in each space between 3dc groups and (3dc, ch3, 3dc) in each corner ch3-sp

Acknowledgements

To my husband Rob and children; Kyra, Oliver and Lulu, I don't think I could have ever taken on a challenge like this without you all beside me cheering me on. Thank you for inspiring and supporting me but most of all thank you for loving me - I feel so honored every day to be a part of your lives.

To my very talented technical editor; Rachel, thank you for always understanding what I mean, even when I struggle to communicate it and for your never-ending positivity and energy. It has been an absolute joy working with you.

To my friend Jo, thank you for being such a supportive friend, always making me laugh and for helping me crochet lots of motifs (and sewing in all those ends!)

A huge thank you to Scheepjes for supplying all the beautiful yarns used in this book.

Last, but not least, thank you to Tuva Publishing for trusting in me and my creativity and allowing my dreams of creating my own book to come true.

Love

Emma